FRONTIERSMEN CAMPING FELLOWSHIP
HANDBOOK

Developed by
ROYAL RANGERS™

Gospel Publishing House
Springfield, Missouri
02-2153

Special thanks to

Fred Deaver, FCF president for some of the information on the American frontiersman, for the story, "A Heap of Trouble," for some of the line drawings, and for the cover art
Dave Howard for the information on frontier clothing
Mickey Click for the information on muzzleloaders
David Barnes for some of the art
Richard Mariott for his line art and redesign
Mike Laliberty for reviewing materials and information for accuracy
Rick Dostal for information on black powder shooting
Brian Hendrickson for compiling the new FCF Trail of the Grizzly into this book

To churches not affiliated with the Assemblies of God: The purchase of Royal Rangers publications and resource items, such as uniforms and accessories, does not grant chartering privileges with the Royal Rangers of the General Council of the Assemblies of God. Neither does such a purchase authorize the purchaser to create or enter a Royal Rangers association with other churches or denominations. Such a purchase allows the function of the ministry within the purchasing church only.

For other Royal Rangers books and supplies, request a *Royal Rangers Catalog* (order number 75-2028). A Royal Rangers order form listing Royal Rangers items available may also be requested (order number 75-2003).

2nd Printing 2004

Printed in the United States of America

CONTENTS

A Tribute to Johnnie Barnes / 5
A Tribute to Fred Deaver / 7

PART 1: The FCF Program / 11

Introduction: The History of FCF / 12
   The Purposes of FCF / 13
   The FCF Motto / 13
   The FCF Symbol / 13
   The FCF Pledge / 14
   The FCF Spirit / 15
   "God's Frontiersmen": An FCF Song / 22
   1. The Organization of FCF / 25
   2. Steps of Recognition in FCF / 30
   3. The Trappers Brigade / 35
   4. The Pathfinder / 41

PART 2: Frontier Traditions and Skills / 45

Introduction: The American Frontiersman / 46
   5. The Frontiersman's Outfit / 53
   6. Leather and Beads / 63
   7. Identification Staffs and Totems / 67
   8. Rifles and Shooting / 71
   9. Powder Horns, Salt Horns, Drinking Cups / 86
   10. Tomahawks and Knives / 91
   11. Fire Starting / 97
   12. Shelter Building / 101
   13. Jerky and Pemmican / 105
   14. Storytelling / 109
Advancement Sign-Off
God's Word for Our Handbook
Glossary

Johnnie Barnes
"Strong Heart"

A Tribute to Johnnie Barnes

God needed a special man to blaze a trail for reaching the boys of the United States. He found that man, a true frontiersman and patriot, in Johnnie Barnes. Not only did God place a vision in Johnnie's heart, but God gave him the needed skills and strength. This strength of heart to see boys won to Jesus Christ earned Johnnie the name "Strong Heart." FCF began as a vision and came to fruition through Johnnie's life poured out before God.

Johnnie pursued excellence in life and demonstrated authenticity in all he did. This led to thousands of boys and men displaying their local heritage in district Rangers camps and Rendezvous of today. When Johnnie traveled, he took time to explore and learn more about our country's heritage. He used this knowledge and the skills God gave him to tell stories and develop authentic period costumes. Yes, Johnnie was a "colorful" man because he took his ministry from God seriously. He knew that boys' lives stood in the balance.

It began with a vision, but Johnnie could only dream that Royal Rangers and FCF would expand all around the world. When he asked me to travel with him in the early 1970s to expand FCF, it gave me an opportunity to see the man, not just the great hero he is for us. I count it a privilege to have worked with Johnnie. We developed a true bond, even closer than brothers. I have described Johnnie with grand words but he would never place himself above others. When some young man or outpost commander approached Johnnie, he was treated as if he were a long lost friend.

I want to thank Johnnie's wife, Juanita, his daughter, Anita, and his son, David. I love them dearly and thank God that I have had the privilege of knowing Johnnie and his family. Royal Rangers remains their legacy as well. Johnnie would be very pleased to see how Royal Rangers and FCF have continued to reach, teach, and keep boys for Jesus Christ.

FRED DEAVER
"HAWKEYE"
NATIONAL FCF PRESIDENT EMERITUS

Fred Deaver
"Hawkeye"
National FCF President Emeritus

A Tribute to Fred Deaver

From the beginning of Royal Rangers, many men worked with the late Johnnie Barnes to establish Royal Rangers in the United States and throughout the world. Most would agree that Fred Deaver's contribution to Royal Rangers is second only to Johnnie Barnes—the founder.

Fred's willingness and commitment to serve in ministry to boys has been consistent for over thirty-five years. Also known as "Mr. Senior Guide," Fred has had a major impact on the lives of thousands of men across America at National Training Camps, teaching the Royal Ranger values and challenging men to become men of God.

Fred has spoken at National Camporama, National FCF Rendezvous, Territorial Rendezvous, District Camporee, and Pow Wow in almost every district in the nation at one time or another.

Fred quickly gives credit to God, as well as to his wife, Joyce, for her tremendous support and confidence that this is "God's will for their life."

Fred Deaver is a recognized artist. He left his employment at Sperry Rand Corporation in the early 1970s to pursue his life's dream as a full-time artist. God has blessed Fred and Royal Rangers with his art. Fred's favorite topics for his art include wildlife, history, the mountain man era of the early 1800s, cowboy scenes, World War I and II airplanes, and still life. Fred was also commissioned by the Boy Scouts to do a portrait of John Wayne, which was presented to the actor in 1978.

Fred, known for his colorful statements and cowboy humor, has always challenged the men to continue to keep the color in Royal Rangers: "This is a ministry to boys! Boys like things that are big and colorful, so don't lose the color—it attracts boys!"

Yes, like many other commanders, it has been my privilege to know Fred and Joyce Deaver. They have spoken to my life many times, and my wife, Lee Anne, and I consider them to be part of our family.

If there ever was a living legend, Fred Deaver qualifies in his own right.

RICHARD MARIOTT
"Razorback"
NATIONAL COMMANDER

7

Richard Mariott
"Razorback"
National Commander

At a special headquarters chapel service, the national Royal Rangers staff presented gifts from Frontiersmen Camping Fellowship chapters and territories from around the United States. These gifts were given to Reverend Thomas Trask, General Superintendent of the Assemblies of God, in appreciation for his support of Royal Rangers and the Frontiersmen Camping Fellowship.

Reverend Trask was to be the Thursday morning speaker at the 2000 FCF National Rendezvous. Just prior to the morning assembly, however, a storm with straight-line winds of over seventy-five miles an hour hit the camp. As a result, the morning assembly was canceled.

FRED DEAVER

PART 1
The FCF Program

Introduction:
The History of FCF

The Frontiersmen Camping Fellowship (FCF, originally called Frontiersmen Camping Fraternity) was founded during the summer of 1966. For some time prior to this, national commander Johnnie Barnes had felt the need for a special honor society to give recognition to older boys and men who had distinguished themselves in advancement, training, and camping.

The early American frontiersmen were an excellent example of people's ability to adapt to the outdoors and the wilderness. Their achievements were also an example of courage and determination. The national Royal Rangers office, therefore, decided to base this fellowship on the lore and traditions of these early frontiersmen.

The first FCF chapter was organized in the Southern California District on July 8, 1966. High in the San Bernardino Mountains, in a clearing surrounded by gigantic trees, a large group of Royal Rangers sat around a blazing campfire. As they waited, a feeling of mystery and expectancy filled the air.

Suddenly, the blast of a hunter's horn shattered the night's stillness and echoed through the trees. National Commander Johnnie Barnes stepped into the firelight dressed in a buckskin outfit and a coonskin cap. As he began to explain the new FCF program, a hum of excitement rose above the sound of the crackling campfire. Assisted by two district leaders, Ron Halvorson and Rob Reid, Commander Barnes proceeded with the first FCF call out. After pledging to endure a time of testing, the candidates were led away carrying a large rope to a mountaintop nearby for an all-night initiation. Later, as the new members (five boys and five men) were officially inducted into the fellowship at the final friendship fire, everyone present sensed that this ceremony was a milestone in Royal Rangers history.

That same year three more FCF chapters were organized, in the Northern California, Southern Missouri, and Iowa Districts. In 1972, the first National Rendezvous was held at Fantastic Caverns near Springfield, Missouri. Two hundred men and boys attended the first Rendezvous. Today, Rendezvous is held every four years, and attendance has grown to one thousand men and boys. Territorial Rendezvous occur every two years, between the National Rendezvous, in each region of the United States. This exciting and unique fellowship has so captured the imaginations of boys and men that the program has grown to include organized chapters in all of our districts.

The Purposes of FCF

1. To give recognition to boys and men who have shown exceptional interest and outstanding achievement in the Royal Rangers program and in Royal Rangers Camp Craft
2. To build a brotherhood of top-notch boys and men who will, over the years, continue to be Royal Rangers program and camping enthusiasts
3. To emphasize the importance of involvement in the advancement program, development of Camp Craft skills, and completion of the leadership training programs
4. To develop a corps of proven Royal Rangers who will strive to be the very best in Christian example and leadership
5. To encourage the boys and men of Royal Rangers to always prefer others above themselves and to let their leadership be by example
6. To show a spirit of servanthood, willing to give of time and energy above and beyond what is expected for Royal Rangers

The FCF Motto

To Give and to Serve (Latin: *Ad Dare Servire*)

The FCF Symbol

The blazing campfire is the official symbol of FCF. The campfire provided the early frontiersmen with light and warmth and was essential for cooking. It was used for other vital needs as well.

The blazing campfire, therefore, symbolizes the spirit of FCF, which is Christian love (warmth), personal witness (light), and dedicated service

The FCF Pledge

I share with you the warmth and glow of this campfire.
These crimson flames are a symbol of our fellowship
and adventures in camping.
I promise to share with you the warmth of Christian friendship
and with others the light of my Christian testimony.
I promise to keep alive the spirit of FCF in my personal life and
to observe at all times the principles of Royal Rangers.

(usefulness). There are five logs around the fire. They represent the five things needed to keep the spirit of FCF alive: courage, achievement, friendship, leadership, and woodsmanship.

The FCF Spirit

FCF endeavors to develop in each member the courageous and undaunted spirit of the early frontiersman. High morale and contagious enthusiasm are developed by urging each member to strive toward five important goals. Each member is encouraged to demonstrate courage, display achievement, develop friendships, demonstrate leadership, and develop woodsmanship.

Courage

Early frontiersmen demonstrated outstanding courage by exploring unknown wilderness; scaling high mountains; crossing barren deserts; blazing trails in virgin forests; and enduring extreme heat, cold, peril, and hardships. Many are the stories of their bravery in battle, their struggle for survival, and their unwavering loyalty in the name of honor. FCF encourages each member to develop this same courageous spirit.

The FCF member must demonstrate courage during his frontier adventure. The work to earn each merit and to participate in the activities of this frontier adventure demands a courageous spirit. He must continue to demonstrate this courage by taking an unwavering stand for the principles of Christianity, by desiring to be the best that he can be for Christ, by bravely enduring each difficulty in life, and by promptly aiding those who need help—even at the risk of his own safety.

Jedidiah Strong Smith was traversing the dry and dangerous Great Basin of Nevada when it became necessary to leave a companion in a shaded area of the desert while he went to find water. Despite danger to himself—even to the point of exhaustion and death—Jedidiah continued on. When he reached water, Jedidiah could have easily forgotten about his partner. But he returned immediately to his companion with the much-needed water. After his companion was refreshed, Jedidiah helped him walk those many miles to the source of that life-saving water. Likewise, each FCF member should strive to be a Jedidiah and lead other boys and men to the source of life-giving water, Jesus of Nazareth.

Achievement

History books are filled with the accounts of outstanding men, such as, Meriwether Lewis and William Clark, Daniel Boone, Davey Crockett, Jedidiah Smith, and Kit Carson. These men carved a name for themselves in our American history through their outstanding achievements. Their undaunted spirit of determination and their desire to excel provide some of the most colorful and exciting pages in our history books.

FCF members should also maintain this desire to excel and achieve. Proficiency in camping and other phases of the Royal Rangers ministry is demonstrated by achieving certain milestones in advancement. These abilities are further demonstrated by each candidate as he completes the Frontier Adventure.

The FCF member should also strive to achieve the following goals: progress in advancement, become more involved in Royal Rangers, and continue to develop skills as a good camper.

Most travel from the East Coast to the West Coast included travel along the Gila River through Arizona. However, in 1827 Jedidiah Smith became the first white man to travel from California to Utah through the Great Basin. Smith discovered what is now known as Ebbetts Pass through the Sierra Nevadas, and he traveled extensively up and down the San Joaquin Valley in central California. Likewise, he traveled into the Rogue and Smith river valleys and took many pelts. Jedidiah became one of the famous trappers and explorers of the West—all before his thirtieth birthday. As a growing and expanding nation, the United States became very interested in the wealth of California and the West because of the knowledge gained during the expeditions of Jedidiah Smith, a strong Christian and true mountain man.

Friendships

The saga of the American frontier contains many accounts of frontiersmen who risked—and sometimes gave—their lives and their fortunes on behalf of their friends. Their unwavering loyalty to friends serves as an inspiration to today's FCF members, who also endeavor to cultivate the same strong bonds of friendship and display the same loyalty to their friends. This feeling of brotherhood is very strong in FCF, and members do their best to uphold this tradition. Through friendships, FCF members fulfill the purpose of preferring others above themselves.

In 1803, President Thomas Jefferson signed an agreement for the United States to purchase a vast untamed and unexplored area. This became known as the Louisiana Purchase. The previous year, Jefferson had begun to plan an exploratory trip to the Pacific Ocean. Jefferson chose Meriwether Lewis to lead the exploration. Lewis was a young man with good outdoor skills, but with little of the scientific knowledge he would need. Among other things, Jefferson taught Lewis botany and the refined navigation skills he would need to complete this daunting task. This strengthened their friendship, which lasted for many years. The preparations continued through 1803 and into 1804. In the spring of 1804, Lewis and Clark, along with their group, headed west. After two years of exploring the West, Lewis and Clark returned to Washington to report on their findings. The friendship and teachings of Thomas Jefferson had helped Lewis to successfully complete his expedition and keep his company safe.

Leadership

Many of today's major highways and mountain passes were once mere trails blazed by early frontiersmen through uncharted wilderness, leading the way for exploration of a new country. Just like a frontiersman, each FCF member should be willing to step out and lead the way by being an  example in Christian living, participating in Christian service, and being willing to assume specific responsibilities. There are still many opportunities awaiting the individual who is willing and ready. An FCF member should prepare himself now for leadership so he will be ready when the opportunity presents itself.

When the beaver industry began to wane in the late 1830s and 1840s, many of the former trappers began farming. Others served as guides for the new pioneers heading west. While many of these mountain men lived in obscurity, one became a national hero. Christopher Houston "Kit" Carson made many trips back and forth from the Missouri Territory to the West. Kit's leadership was best demonstrated not by his actions and many accomplishments, but rather by the goodness and the justice with which he

treated those under his care. He served as an Indian agent for a number of years and was highly respected by the Native Americans under his care. He treated them with the care and respect that any person should receive and did much to bring favor to the Native American peoples, especially the Utes. Kit participated in a number of rendezvous in the 1830s. He continued to serve in leadership as a Union officer during the Civil War. Rivers, passes, and the capital of Nevada were named after Kit Carson, but his greatest achievement was the leadership he provided for so many people.

Woodsmanship

Early frontiersmen were able to adapt to almost any wilderness situation because they were constantly developing outdoor skills. It became a matter of survival to know what to do and how to do it. As experienced woodsmen, they could spend months on the frontier with only a small knapsack, a blanket, a rifle, and a hunting knife. Today's FCF member should also continue to develop outdoor skills. He should use every opportunity available to demonstrate these skills in a camping situation. An FCF member should not only be a trained woodsman, but also an experienced woodsman.

The Hudson's Bay Company ruled the fur trading industry in the Northwest for many years, but the introduction of the American mountain man to the West was considered a tremendous threat to their holdings. It has been claimed that the one million square miles of the untamed West was inhabited by only one thousand adventurous men, yet the skill and determination of these men caused consternation on the part of the Hudson's Bay Company. These men were able to endure grizzly bear attacks, often performing field surgery on the wounded without any medical training. They were able to survive the brutal winters and harsh weather that frequented the High Sierra and Rocky Mountains with the barest of equipment and supplies. Very few men became rich, but many became famous for their skills, abilities, and fortitude.

GOD'S FRONTIERSMEN

AN FCF SONG

Ed Leonard

D   G   D

1. Out where the riv - ers wind thru the land,
2. Like the fron - tiers - men, on - ward we ride;
3. Out where the te - pees reach to the sky,
4. Some day will come when God's work will be done;

5   G   D   A7

once rode fron - tiers - men, time and a - gain;
"REA - DY" for bat - tle, God's Word at our side;
'round the warm camp - fire sit you and I;
home - ward with Je - sus, the bat - tle is won;

9   D   G   D

Rea - dy for dan - gers, brave and se - cure;
though there are dan - gers, we are se - cure;
bro - thers in Je - sus, with one ac - cord;
we'll trade our te - pees, rag - ged and old, for

13   G   D   A7   D

Carv - ing a na - tion that would en - dure.
We're God's Fron - tiers - men, we will en - dure. *) GO TO CHORUS*
We're God's Fron - tiers - men, praising the Lord.
one of God's man - sions that's made of gold.

18 D   G   D

Chorus :

WE'RE GOD'S FRON - TIERS - MEN, RI - DING TO - DAY

22 G   D   A7

LIV - ING FOR JE - SUS, POINT - ING THE WAY;

26 D   G   D

CAMP - ING IN TE - PEES, BUCK - SKINS AND ALL ;

30 G   D   A7   D

WE'RE GOD'S FRON - TIERS - MEN, ANS-WERING THE CALL.

Royal Rangers
Frontiersmen Camping
Organizational Chart

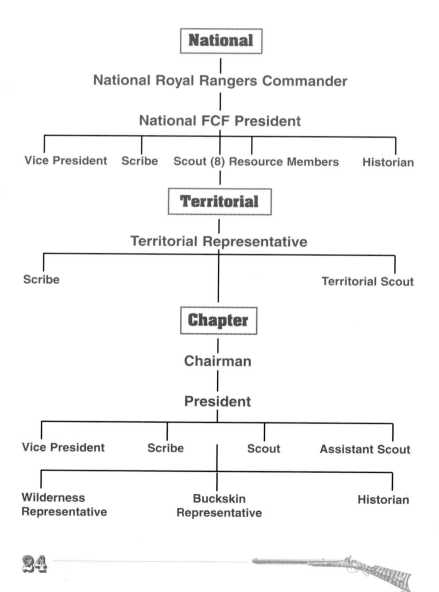

National

National Royal Rangers Commander

National FCF President

| Vice President | Scribe | Scout (8) Resource Members | Historian |

Territorial

Territorial Representative

Scribe   Territorial Scout

Chapter

Chairman

President

| Vice President | Scribe | Scout | Assistant Scout |

| Wilderness Representative | Buckskin Representative | Historian |

Chapter 1
The Organization of FCF District Chapters

ach chapter elects or appoints, per their bylaws, its own officers, with the exception of chairman; the district commander becomes chairman by virtue of his office. Chapter officers are president, vice president, and scribe. A district scout and assistant scout, from among the boys, serve on the chapter staff. They are selected through a popular vote after they have demonstrated their skills and knowledge.

Chapter Name

To further emphasize the traditions of FCF, each district chapter selects a historical name. This could be the name of a famous frontiersman from the area, an Indian tribe, a historical site, or a geographical location that played an important role in the state's history. For example, the chapter in the Southern Missouri District is the Daniel Boone Chapter.

Chapter Trace

The chapter should plan several special events for the FCF members each year. These events should be some type of rugged outdoor adventure designed to be colorful and challenging. At least one event per year should be the "Chapter Trace." The Chapter Trace, or Chapter Business Meeting, is the time for the chapter's annual business sessions and elections.

Regions

The Royal Rangers program is divided into eight geographical regions. Each region is supervised by a regional coordinator. The regional coordinator is also the regional FCF chairman.

Territories

To further assist in the promotion and development of FCF, the eight regions are used in FCF and called territories: Trappers

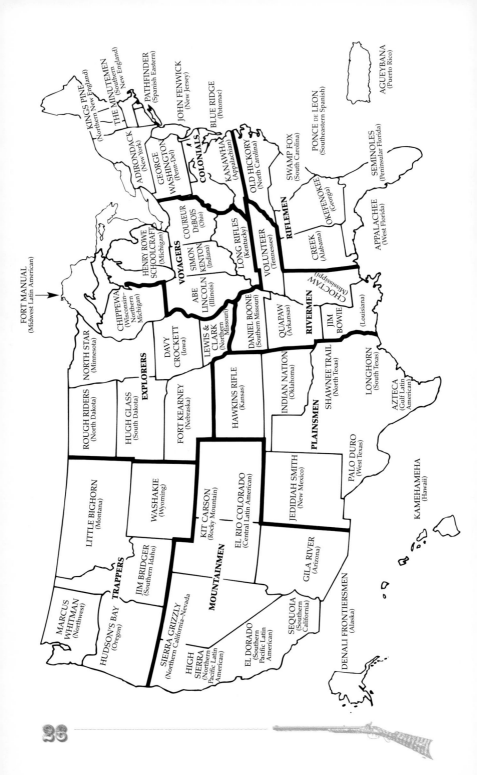

FORT MANUAL
(Midwest Latin American)

KINGS PINE
(Northern New England)
THE MINUTEMEN
(Southern New England)
PATHFINDER
(Spanish Eastern)
JOHN FENWICK
(New Jersey)
BLUE RIDGE
(Potomac)
AGUEYBANA
(Puerto Rico)

ADIRONDACK
(New York)
GEORGE WASHINGTON
(Penn-Del)
COLONIALS
KANAWHA
(Appalachian)
OLD HICKORY
(North Carolina)
SWAMP FOX
(South Carolina)
PONCE DE LEON
(Southeastern Spanish)
SEMINOLES
(Peninsular Florida)

HENRY ROWE SCHOOLCRAFT
(Michigan)
COUREUR DeBOIS
(Ohio)
VOYAGERS
SIMON KENTON
(Indiana)
LONG RIFLES
(Kentucky)
VOLUNTEER
(Tennessee)
RIFLEMEN
OKEFENOKEE
(Georgia)
CREEK
(Alabama)
APPALACHEE
(West Florida)

CHIPPEWA
(Wisconsin-Northern Michigan)
ABE LINCOLN
(Illinois)
CHOCTAW
(Mississippi)
(Louisiana)

NORTH STAR
(Minnesota)
DAVY CROCKETT
(Iowa)
LEWIS & CLARK
(Northern Missouri)
DANIEL BOONE
(Southern Missouri)
QUAPAW
(Arkansas)
RIVERMEN
JIM BOWIE

EXPLORERS

ROUGH RIDERS
(North Dakota)
HUGH GLASS
(South Dakota)
FORT KEARNEY
(Nebraska)
HAWKINS RIFLE
(Kansas)
INDIAN NATION
(Oklahoma)
SHAWNEE TRAIL
(North Texas)
LONGHORN
(South Texas)
PLAINSMEN
PALO DURO
(West Texas)
AZTECA
(Gulf Latin American)
KAMEHAMEHA
(Hawaii)

LITTLE BIGHORN
(Montana)
WASHAKIE
(Wyoming)
KIT CARSON
(Rocky Mountain)
EL RIO COLORADO
(Central Latin American)
JEDIDIAH SMITH
(New Mexico)

TRAPPERS
JIM BRIDGER
(Southern Idaho)
GILA RIVER
(Arizona)
MOUNTAINMEN
DENALI FRONTIERSMEN
(Alaska)

MARCUS WHITMAN
(Northwest)
HUDSON'S BAY
(Oregon)
SIERRA GRIZZLY
(Northern California–Nevada)
HIGH SIERRA
(Northern Pacific Latin American)
EL DORADO
(Southern Pacific Latin American)
SEQUOIA
(Southern California)

26

(Northwest), Mountainmen (Southwest), Explorers (North
Central), Plainsmen (South Central), Voyagers (Great Lakes),
Rivermen (Gulf), Colonials (Northeast), and Riflemen (Southeast).
An FCF territorial representative is appointed by the national
Royal Rangers commander to serve each of these territories. A territorial scout and a scribe represent the boys of Royal Rangers age
in each territory.

Territorial Rendezvous

Each territory has
a Rendezvous every
two years. A
Rendezvous is an
outdoor event that
includes a black
powder shoot, tomahawk throwing,
knife throwing, a
best outfit contest,
flint and steel fire
building, trading,
learning of new
skills, crafts, and
other frontier-related
activities.
Advancement into
Buckskin and
Wilderness are also
commonly held at
the Territorial
Rendezvous.

National Positions

To give national recognition to the program and to further
assist in its development, a national FCF president and vice president are appointed. The president's term of office is two years. A
national scribe and a national historian are appointed by the
national president. The national scouts represent the boys in the
total FCF program. The eight regional scouts and assistant scouts

are elected at the Territorial Rendezvous and the national scouts and assistant scouts are elected at the National FCF Rendezvous or the National Camporama. They wear the national staff patch during their term in office. Their term of office is two years.

National FCF Rendezvous

A National FCF Rendezvous is conducted every four years. This outstanding event includes not only the activities of the Territorial Rendezvous, but also a number of colorful ceremonies, pageants, special features, unusual services, and outstanding speakers.

1972 Rendezvous
Fantastic Caverns, MO

1976 Rendezvous
Blue Eye, MO

1980 Rendezvous
Cumberland Gap, TN

1984 Rendezvous
Hungry Horse, MT

1988 Rendezvous
Eagle Rock, MO

1992 Rendezvous
Eagle Rock, MO

1996 Rendezvous
Eagle Rock, MO

2000 Rendezvous
Eagle Rock, MO

2004 Rendezvous
Eagle Rock, MO

Chapter 2
Steps of Recognition in FCF

Young Bucks are Frontiersmen Camping Fellowship members who are in grades six through twelve (eleven through seventeen years old). Old-Timers are FCF members who are eighteen and over.

The Trail of the Grizzly

The "Trail of the Grizzly" is designed to lead boys and leaders along the challenging FCF advancement trail. The purpose of this Trail is to prepare boys and leaders to successfully complete each of the FCF advancements by including a unique set of merit award requirements for the Frontiersmen, Buckskin, and Wilderness steps.

All Trail of the Grizzly merit awards are easily identified with a grizzly paw print. The Frontiersmen merit awards display a green grizzly paw on the merit. The Buckskin merit awards display a black grizzly paw on the merit, and the Wilderness merit awards display a white grizzly paw.

See the form "Advancement Sign-Off" at the back of this book for keeping track of advancement progress.

Both Boys and Leaders

○ Earn the following merit awards: Rope Craft, Fire Craft,

Cooking, Compass, Lashing, First Aid Skills, Camping, and Tool Craft.
- ○ Explain the plan of salvation.
- ○ Explain the meaning of the four red points, four gold points, and eight blue points of the Royal Rangers Emblem.

Boys Only

- ○ Be at least eleven years old and at least an Adventure Ranger.
- ○ Be recommended by the outpost commander.

Leaders Only

- ○ Complete the Rangers Basics module of the Leadership Training Academy.
- ○ Be a Royal Rangers leader in good standing with your church.

Both Boys and Leaders

After earning all eight required merits, you have earned the Grizzly Trail FCF Merit Award. You are now eligible for the Frontier Adventure. After successful completion, you will receive your Frontiersmen Pin.

Both Boys and Leaders

- ○ Earn the following merit awards: Church, Knife and Hawk, and Black Powder or Archery.
- ○ Participate in at least one Frontier Adventure. (This does not include your Frontier Adventure you participated in to become a Frontiersman.)
- ○ Make, trade, or purchase a complete FCF outfit.
- ○ Recite from memory the FCF Pledge.

○ Explain the meaning of the FCF Symbol.
○ State the vision and purpose of FCF.
○ Make an FCF identification staff.
○ Select a frontier-related craft or skill to develop.
○ Select an FCF name.
○ Complete the Buckskin workbook.
○ Be an active member in good standing for at least one year.

Boys Only

○ Earn the Bronze Medal or one Expedition Ranger Medal.

Leaders Only

○ Sponsor a boy into FCF.
○ Earn the Leader's Medal of Achievement.

Both Boys and Leaders

After earning the additional three required merits and completing the Buckskin study program, submit your application for advancement to Buckskin to the district FCF office. After successful completion of the Buckskin testing, you will be awarded your Buckskin Pin at a special ceremony.

Both Boys and Leaders

○ Earn the following merit awards: Christian Service, Wilderness Survival, Primitive Snares, and Primitive Shelters.
○ Complete the Wilderness workbook.

Boys Only

○ Earn the Silver Medal or a second Expedition Ranger Medal.
○ Sponsor a boy into FCF.
○ Participate in at least two Frontier Adventures, and be an active member in good standing for at least two years.

Leaders Only

○ Attend a National Training Camp.
○ Sponsor an additional boy into FCF.
○ Participate in four Frontier Adventures. (This does not include the Frontier Adventure you participated in to become a Frontiersman, but it does include the Buckskin required Frontier Adventure.)

Both Boys and Leaders

After earning the additional four required merits and completing the Wilderness study program, submit your application for advancement to Wilderness to the district FCF office. Then wear the Wilderness Pouch until the Vigil is completed. After successful completion of the Wilderness Vigil, you will be awarded your Wilderness Pin during a special ceremony.

FRONTIER PREACHER

Chapter 3

The Trappers Brigade

The purpose of the Trappers Brigade is to promote Christian service among the FCF members by encouraging their involvement and participation in service to their church and fellowman.

The Trappers Brigade encourages the involvement of FCF members not only in their local church, but also in their community (e.g., needs, projects, and organizations), in this way extending their Christian influence and testimony.

To participate in the Trappers Brigade program an FCF member

1. Must be in good standing with his FCF chapter.
2. Must have paid his current and previous year's dues.
3. Must have participated in one-half of the district FCF activities during the current and previous year.
4. Must be actively involved in his local church and Royal Rangers outpost.

The FCF member need not have received his Buckskin or Wilderness status to qualify.

Service Points

Service points are accumulated when an FCF member volunteers his time (with no consideration for wages) in church, in community projects, in special needs organizations, or in humanitarian acts. Young Bucks will receive one point per hour of service. This does not include travel time. An Old-Timer will receive one-half point per hour of service done within the community where he resides. For volunteer work done outside of his local setting, he will accumulate one point per hour of service, not counting travel time. He continues to add his total points together even after he has attained the next step. Projects are determined by the FCF Trappers Brigade Authorization Committee.

THE OLD TIMER & YOUNG'N

Service Projects

Within the local church, service projects may include mowing the church lawn; visiting the sick; serving as an usher; teaching or helping in Sunday School; participating in youth, bus, or music ministry; doing office work or printing; and participating in missions emphasis, fund-raising, or clothing or food drives.

Within the local community, projects may include helping families who have lost their homes because of a disaster (e.g., fire, tornado, or flood); assisting needy people or children's groups; working with a hospital, library, service center, voter registration drive, city recreational facility, juvenile detention center, the Big Brothers organization, or the Boys and Girls Club.

Outside the local setting, the member may accumulate points (not counting travel time) for missionary trips with MAPS (Missions Abroad Placement Service), FCF Pathfinder missions projects (see the next chapter for details), missionary trips with AIM (Ambassadors in Missions), AGHM (Assemblies of God Home Missions) projects, Convoy of Hope projects, AGWM (Assemblies of God World Missions) projects, CARE Corps projects, USO (United Service Organizations) projects, disaster assistance, search-and-rescue missions, etc. Check with your district commander for other considerations.

Steps of Recognition

The three steps of recognition and the accumulated points needed to attain them are as follows:

○ Company Trapper—20 total points
○ Bourgeois (pronounced boohz-wah')—60 total points
○ Free Trapper—120 total points

For each additional thirty points earned, the Free Trapper will receive a numeral to be placed on his Trapper Medal.

A District FCF Authorization Committee will review the points tabulated by the FCF members who qualify for recognition pins. Each FCF member needs to complete an application and be interviewed by the committee. During the interview the FCF member will share the details of his service project. Pictures, letters, artifacts, items of interest, and things learned, enjoyed, or experienced should all be shared when meeting with the committee.

Young Bucks must complete the service under the supervision of an adult leader. The leader may be a pastor, youth leader, commander, community leader, missionary, district official, project coordinator, coach, parent, or any other adult who can sign the application and verify what was done by the applicant. See the sample card below.

Old-Timers may earn points in two ways: through service and through supervising Young Bucks during their Trappers Brigade service projects. The Old-Timer will earn five points for each step of recognition completed by a boy he has supervised. The Old-Timer must sign the Young Buck's application as his supervisor and send appropriate comments with the application. He must also participate with the Young Buck and organize and motivate the Young Buck's participation to complete the service project, seeing that the project is completed while the Young Buck is under eighteen years old.

FCF Trapper's Brigade Points Record

Name of Project	Location/Date	Type of Work	Initials By Sponsor	Points
1.				
2.				
3.				
4.				
5.				
6.				
7.				
8.				
9.				
10.				

Medal Awarded   Date _____   Total Points _____

Company Trapper–20 points, **Bourgeois**–60 points, **Free Trapper**–120 points

Each additional 30 points will entitle the Free Trapper to receive a numeral to be placed on his Trapper Brigade medal.

TRAPPER BRIGADE PINS

(To be worn behind FCF Membership Pin)

COMPANY TRAPPER

BOURGEOIS

FREE TRAPPER

Chapter 4
Pathfinders

Pathfinders ministry was born in the heart of Paul Etheridge, a Royal Ranger and fellow FCFer, to provide work teams for needy places where many other MAPS teams are unable to go. This focus does not change; Pathfinders continues to provide teams to accomplish these most difficult projects. To help promote Royal Rangers involvement at all levels of AGHM and AGWM MAPS projects, one identifiable name was needed. Pathfinders is that name and has three categories: Bronze, Silver and Gold trips.

Royal Rangers Pathfinders provides teams to meet needs in Mission America Placement Service (AGHM MAPS) and Missions Abroad Placement Service (AGWM MAPS). The most difficult MAPS projects go and serve where other teams are unable to go because of primitive conditions. (The most difficult projects are now known as the *Gold Pathfinder*. These Gold Pathfinder projects will continue to be a primary focus.)

VISION: Royal Rangers participating in AGHM and AGWM MAPS projects through Bronze, Silver, and Gold Pathfinders approved trips.

PURPOSE:

○ Royal Rangers participation in AGHM and AGWM MAPS projects.

○ To make propagation of the gospel possible in all areas of the world by assisting in MAPS construction projects.

○ To retain the current Pathfinders mission "To Go Where No One Will Go" type of projects.

○ To provide additional credit for AGHM projects and regular AGWM Maps projects.

○ To develop a closer working relationship between AGHM MAPS, AGWM MAPS and the national Royal Rangers ministry.

○ To encourage others to become involved in a home and world missions benevolent service

WHO CAN PARTICIPATE:
Participants in all three categories can be Royal Rangers, FCFers and skilled non-Royal Rangers approved by their pastor and by AGHM or AGWM office.

Pathfinders

Royal Rangers who participate in any of the three categories may wear the appropriate Pathfinders pin on their uniform or awards vest per the uniform guide. To qualify for the Pathfinder award, the member must participate in a mission that meets the criteria listed below.

Bronze: AGHM MAPS trips within the United States. The Path-finders pin has a bronze world on the pin to identify this category.

○ The project must be approved through the AGHM MAPS office and have a project number.

○ Projects must have prior approval of the national Royal Rangers office.

○ The AGHM MAPS project must be outside of your home district to qualify. Projects within your home district are given Trappers Brigade credit.

Silver: AGHM or AGWM MAPS trips with your church, or any team approved by the MAPS office and national Royal Rangers office. The Pathfinders pin has a silver world on the pin to identify this category.

○ The project must be approved through the MAPS office and have a project number.

○ Projects must have prior approval of the district office and the national Royal Rangers office.

○ The mission must be at least five days long, not including travel time.

Gold: The phrase "To go where no one else will go" is an appropriate missions statement. These are experienced tradesmen and individuals who choose a difficult project to complete. The project may include hiking, backpacking, boating, or canoeing to out-of-the-way locations that may not have electricity or other modern conditions. The Gold Project coordinator will evaluate these projects. The Pathfinders pin has a gold world on the pin to identify this category.

○ The Pathfinders Gold projects must also be approved by the AGWM MAPS office and national Royal Rangers office.

○ The project must be the type most other groups would not attempt because of remote location, hardship, or required campcraft skills. To provide teams for difficult projects typically not done by other church teams.

Additional Pathfinders Award Information

Because Pathfinders assignments must be regulated by the MAPS offices, some restrictions apply. For example, no person under 14 may go outside the United States unless accompanied by a parent or a guardian.

The administration of the Pathfinders program is conducted by the national Royal Rangers office, AGHM and AGWM Pathfinders coordinators, and the national Pathfinders committee. For more information, contact the national Royal Rangers office. This enables the various groups planning a trip to promote their trip throughout the United States and provide greater communication between AGHM and AGWM MAPS, the national Royal Rangers office, and the missionaries in the field.

PART 2
Frontier Traditions and Skills

Introduction:
The American Frontiersman

The history of the United States is filled with accounts of men who contributed to the development of our nation. A special breed of man in the long list of our country's forefathers was the old frontiersman. He was among the most colorful characters in American history, and he played a vital role in widening the borders of our land. He tamed virgin territory, making it safer for those who followed.

The Frontiersman's Equipment

This rugged pioneer, like the modern astronaut, depended on his life-support equipment as he left the last settlement to explore the unknown. He usually wore buckskin, which was an ideal material for wilderness living. It was readily available and fairly easy to work with. It was windproof, rainproof, and virtually snag proof. It took years to wear out. The frontiersman usually wore leather moccasins, which he replaced quite often. Headgear included a coonskin cap, a wide-brimmed hat, a tricorn hat, or whatever else suited his fancy.

The frontiersman carried a good rifle. It had two functions: to protect him and, most importantly, to supply him with food and clothing. Along with the rifle, the frontiersman carried a rifle case made of buckskin. These cases were often decorated with fringe and beadwork or quillwork.

In a hunting bag the frontiersman carried a pouch containing rifle balls, extra flints, a powder measure, a ball starter, and a roll of pillow ticking for patches. He may have carried a few extra parts to repair his rifle, just in case it broke down. He probably carried a mainspring, a screw or two, a tool kit, and maybe a screwdriver or a pick to clean the flashhole. On a strap of his hunting bag he kept a small, sharp knife, called a patch cutter or patch knife.

If he had a flintlock rifle, the frontiersman usually carried two powder horns. He had a small horn full of FFFFg (4-Fg) flash powder for the pan and a large horn that held one to one and a half pounds of FFg (2-Fg) or FFFg (3-Fg) powder for the main charge.

The frontiersman also carried a knife on his belt, more than likely a butcher knife. Slipped on the back of the belt was a good tomahawk. Tucked over the belt in the front was another pouch called a possibles bag. In it he carried flint and steel, along with a container of tinder to catch a spark to make a fire. Also in this pouch he may have had a small horn full of salt, some jerky, pemmican, or parched corn to snack on, as well as personal items. If he had a packhorse, he carried many extra things to make his life in the unknown wilderness much easier.

Many adventuresome men who left for the wilderness in the early days of this country never made it back. Only those who took care of their equipment and knew how to use it had any chance of survival. There is an old saying that still holds true today: "Take care of your equipment, and it will take care of you."

The Rendezvous

During the early 1800s, the beaver hat was in fashion. This created a great demand for beaver pelts. Consequently, the mountains in the West soon swarmed with men who trapped the beaver for selling and shipping back East (the trapping era occurred between 1804 and 1840). These men were a special breed of frontiersmen—the mountain men.

As they trapped the beaver, mountain men adopted the ways of the Native Americans. They adapted to life in the mountains and the wilderness so well that most were reluctant to return to civilization. However, they needed a market for their furs, as well as a source for replenishing their supplies (salt, gunpowder, etc.) and replacing equipment (traps, pots, axes, etc.).

To meet this need of the mountain men, certain traders from back East traveled west into the mountains to a predetermined location, or "rendezvous" (from the French). They traded their supplies for the mountain men's furs. Because the mountain man had little need for money, he took most of the price of his furs in trade goods. Thus, the famous rendezvous was born.

The site of the rendezvous was usually in a valley where there was a good stream and plenty of grass for grazing. The traders would arrive first, their wagons and packhorses laden with trade goods.

Soon, from out of the mountains all over the West, the mountain men would come. Clad in their best buckskins, they would approach the rendezvous at a full gallop, whooping and shooting their guns in the air. There would be lots of shouting and back-slapping when they spied an old friend.

The Native American wives of many of the mountain men would soon have the valley dotted with colorful tepees. Many friendly Native Americans also attended, adding to the color.

Most of these mountain men lived rather isolated lives, so they would determine to make this the one big event of the year. Many were eager to demonstrate their improved skills, so there were contests of various kinds, from horse racing to black powder shooting. Huge cooking pots of food would be emptied, and laughter, shouting, and singing would echo throughout the valley long into the night. They would share new adventures or retell old ones, or perhaps give a tribute to a friend who didn't live to make it to that rendezvous.

Notable mountain men such as Jim Bridger, Jedidiah Strong Smith, John Colter, Kit Carson, Joseph Meek, and Hugh Glass attended these rendezvous. Only sixteen rendezvous were held, with the first occurring in 1825 and the last in 1840. However, the rendezvous were an important part of American history because they brought explorers and frontiersmen to the vast, untamed wilderness. This provided a stepping stone for the settlers to follow. In fact, many mountain men became guides for the burgeoning thousands who made their way to the West in later years.

The rendezvous sometimes attracted individuals other than traders, Native Americans, and mountain men. Famous frontier preachers, artists, and historians were also among those who attended, and they left us their versions of the events in writings and drawings.

Many historians agree that these rendezvous were the most colorful events ever held in the West. When the beaver trade died and the last rendezvous was held, a great frontier tradition vanished. However, today's frontiersmen in FCF are reviving this tradition in the Territorial and National Rendezvous. Appreciation for these colorful Americans was one of the reasons the national Royal Rangers office selected the frontier theme as a basis for the Frontiersmen Camping Fellowship.

Many of the skills and crafts of our forefathers are fast

disappearing from the American scene. One of the goals of FCF is to master and preserve these skills and pass them on to others. The following chapters contain some of the frontier skills an FCF member may develop. It is not necessary to obtain all the items discussed. However, you should make or obtain some of them to create an outfit with a more authentic look.

FD

CRIZZ

Chapter 5
The Frontiersman's Outfit

Headgear

Frontiersmen wore a variety of headgear, from the headdress used by the Native Americans to the store-bought felt or beaver hat. Many hats were made out of furs the frontiersmen acquired from skunk, raccoon, fox, coyote, cougar, deer, and bear.

Hats were shaped and then decorated to the individual's taste using feathers and hatbands. Several had leather visors, or bills. Some were made out of wamus (a strong, rough cloth), wool, or linen with fur added to them. Some different types of hats included the round hat, tricorn hat, felt hat, Canadian cap, top hat, derby, fur hat, coonskin cap, leather hat, and beaver hat. Many of the mountain men wore beaver hats in honor of the animals that had provided them with their most valuable trading furs.

Many a mountain man, after selling all his hides in the spring, went on a buying fling. Sometimes he bought city clothes, such as a white shirt with a stiff collar, a black suit with long split tails, and a derby or a stovepipe hat. When he headed back to the

mountains—back in his skins—it was not uncommon for him to still be wearing his city hat.

Shirts

The shirts worn by the frontiersmen varied from region to region. The materials used to make shirts included buckskin, elk-skin, buffalo, calico, linen, wool, wamus, and cotton duck. Jedidiah Smith usually bought each of his men two or three yards of calico so they could make their own shirts.

A frontiersman was not away from civilization for long before he wore out the clothing he had brought from home. He then had to make clothing from whatever he could find. Generally he used buckskin. Most of his shirts had fringe on them, which helped drain off the rain. The fringe was also a ready source of binding thongs.

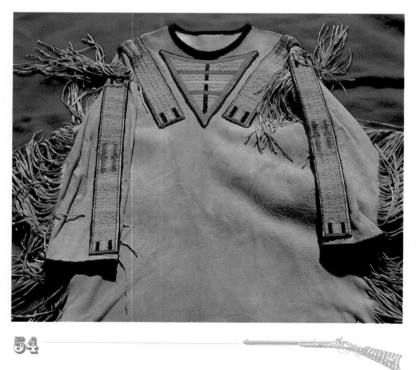

Many shirts were decorated with beadwork, painted designs, and other items. Some different types of shirts found on the frontier were the French shirt, colonial shirt, waistcoat (somewhat like a vest), calico shirt, rifle frock, Plains Indian shirt, and trapper's shirt.

Making a Buckskin-Style Shirt

Shirts may be made from deerskin, elkskin, or similar material. Try to make your shirt look authentic. These instructions are for a buckskin-style shirt as pictured on page 54 and 56.

1. Carefully take apart an old shirt and use it as a pattern to cut out the material. (Patterns for shirts and other clothing may also be purchased.)
2. When cutting out the front and back pieces, make them slightly longer than a regular shirt to allow for fringe.
3. Cut an opening in the front piece (see the illustration) and finish off the edges. Punch several holes on either side of the opening. Thread a leather string through the holes to hold together the opening.

4. Stitch the shoulder seams together.

5. Attach the collar. Shirts may also be made without a collar (as the Indian-style shirt pictured on page 54), or they may be split all the way down the front and worn like a coat.

6. Stitch in the sleeves.

7. Stitch up the side seams, leaving a three-inch slit on each side at the bottom of the shirt.

8. Attach additional strips of leather fringe to the front, back, and sleeves.

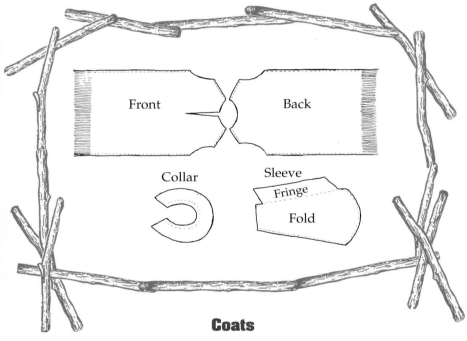

Coats

Coats and robes were a must during cold weather. Some of these coats were brought from home, but most were made on the frontier. Some coats did not have sleeves on them and protected only the body. They were made from the same kinds of materials as shirts.

Some fur coats were worn with the fur inside for warmth and the hide outside for rain protection. A coat made out of a blanket was called a "capote." These generally were made from a three and a half-point Hudson Bay or Whitney blanket. Knee-length coats made from cloth were called cassocks.

In addition to coats, there were robes. These robes were made from larger animals, such as buffalo, elk, bear, and moose. Usually these robes still had the hair on them and were wrapped around the body for warmth. They were also used as blankets.

Sometimes a cape or yoke was worn during cool weather. This was a piece of buckskin worn over the shoulders.

Pants and Leggings

Pants on the frontier were simple and plain. It was not until late in the days of the frontier that pockets were added to pants. The materials used for pants were usually linen, wamus, cotton duck, and leather. The types of pants worn were overalls (not like today's overalls), trousers, mountain man pants, and buffalo hunter pants (which were made of buffalo hide).

On the eastern frontier one might have seen knee-length breeches, which were made out of cloth. Some pants were decorated with beadwork.

Sometimes a frontiersman wore leggings. Leggings were two separate pants legs without a midsection. They were held up by a leather strap tied to a sash or belt (perhaps the forerunners of chaps). Breechcloths, or breechclouts, made from a variety of materials, were worn with leggings to give protection to the mid-section. They were tucked under the sash or belt in the back and front. (Leggings are not to be confused with gaiters, described under "Footwear.") It is not always appropriate to wear leggings and breechcloths at FCF Rendezvous and events.

Footwear

The moccasin was the chief footwear on the frontier. Moccasins were made from different kinds of leather. Some were decorated ornately, others were plain. When moccasins wore out, instead of throwing them away, the frontiersman would often make a new pair and wear them on top of the old pair. While the cobbler was still making the square-toed boot or shoe to be worn on either foot, Native Americans were making a moccasin for the left foot and a moccasin for the right foot.

Square-toed shoes with large buckles were common on the eastern frontier. Also, boots with square or rounded toes were often seen. However, once these boots or shoes wore out, western frontiersmen had to change to moccasins.

Gaiters (also known as botas) were also worn for added protection to the lower leg and ankle. They were made of leather, wamus, or cotton duck. They were worn over the pants from the knee down and covered the instep.

Assembling the FCF Outfit

1. Patches were not a part of the frontier outfit. In keeping with an authentic look, they should not be part of the FCF outfit. This includes Royal Rangers district camp patches and chapter FCF patches.
2. To keep the simple, hand-crafted look, no tooled leatherwork on belts or other items should be worn. Beadwork and quillwork

are always encouraged to make the item more ornate.

3. It is illegal to possess any part of any raptor. Therefore, no claws or feathers from eagles, owls, hawks, or other such animals may be part of the FCF outfit.

4. Be aware that bear claws are not to be bought or sold unless state regulations permit it.

5. Any buttons on FCF clothing should be made from materials that were available during that time period: horn, wood, leather, shell (not metallic cartridges), pewter, or brass. Coins were sometimes made into buttons during frontier times.

6. In keeping with the frontier character, avoid zippers if possible.

Chapter 6
Leather and Beads

Leather

Much of what frontiersmen wore or used, such as their shirts, pants, coats, moccasins, belts, capes, pouches, leggings, knife sheaths, and gun cases, was fashioned in some way from leather or skins. Most of these items can be handmade by the Frontiersmen Camping Fellowship member.

The shooting pouch, sometimes called a hunting pouch, was used to carry items for shooting. It was generally made of leather and usually contained the following items: a small shot pouch (containing rifle balls), extra flints or percussion caps, material (for example, pillow ticking) for making patches, tools for cleaning or working on the rifle, spare parts, a powder measure, and a ball starter. On one of the shoulder straps of his shooting pouch was a sheath containing a small, sharp patch knife used for cutting off surplus patch material. Sometimes these pouches were decorated with beadwork and other items.

In addition to a shooting pouch, the frontiersman sometimes carried a possibles bag (personal pouch). Because his trousers had no pockets, this pouch was used to carry items normally carried in pockets. It probably contained his firebox (flint and steel), tinder, jerky, pemmican, parched corn, and other personal items. These pouches were usually made from pliable leather or skins. Sometimes they were decorated with quillwork, beadwork, or paintings. Making a shooting pouch or possibles bag by hand is an excellent project for every FCF member.

The early frontiersman made a buckskin case to protect his rifle when not in use. Such cases were usually decorated with fringe and bead-work. He also made a capper. A capper was a device made from a heavy piece of leather that was punched with small holes to hold percussion caps for a percussion rifle.

Capper

Many leather-craft stores supply materials and patterns for many of the items mentioned above. A number of craft books also give details on how to make them.

Working With Leather

Here are a few tips to help you develop your leather-craft skills.

1. Obtain the proper tools and materials. You will probably need a leather cutter, a cutting board, a leather punch, and a lacing needle—or a leather awl if you prefer stitching instead of lacing. You will also need sufficient leather, lacing or wax thread, and some type of pattern.

2. Get the most out of your leather. A lot of valuable leather is lost by improper cutting. Place your pattern in various positions until you find the combination that will leave the least amount of wasted material.

3. Mark the outline of your pattern on the unexposed side of the

leather or buckskin. This is easier than pinning the pattern to the material. Always double-check pattern lines before cutting. Sometimes it is a good idea to pin together the paper pattern to be sure it is the right size before you cut out the leather.

4. It is much easier to do a job neatly if you temporarily glue the seams together before you lace or stitch. However, be careful and do not allow any of the glue to show on the exposed surface. Glue has a tendency to change the color of the leather.

5. Buckskin has a tendency to stretch. Keep this in mind when working with it.

Beads

Some frontiersmen decorated their clothing, pouches, moccasins, gun cases, and belts with Native American beadwork. This beadwork was not added to their work clothes, but to the clothing they wore on special occasions, such as the rendezvous.

If you wish to decorate some of your personal items, beaded strips and pieces of various shapes of leather may be purchased from many Native American handcraft shops. However, many FCF members make their own beadwork. If you would like to give this a try, a number of handcraft shops have the beads and other materials you will need to learn the art of beadwork.

Chapter 7
Identification Staffs and Totems

Identification Staffs

Early frontiersmen and Native Americans often made a unique staff that marked their claims. During hunts, for example, these staffs were driven into the ground beside slain animals to show ownership. They were also placed in front of cabins and lodges to identify the owner.

In the Frontiersmen Camping Fellowship, these staffs are carried by members during FCF activities, placed in front of their shelters during outings and district camps, and driven into the ground in front of the member during FCF campfire ceremonies. These unique staffs have become a very colorful addition to FCF ceremonies and activities.

The staffs are typically three feet long with a pointed end to stick into the ground. But staffs can be made up to six feet long and can be used as walking sticks. The ends may have flint or metal points to stick into the ground. Each FCF member should create his own design by carving, painting, or attaching feathers, beads, etc. (See also page 68.)

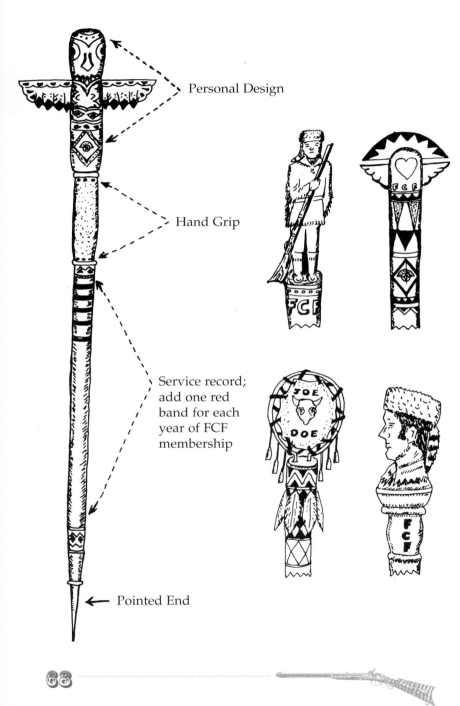

Personal Design

Hand Grip

Service record;
add one red
band for each
year of FCF
membership

Pointed End

JOE

DOE

FCF

FCF

FCF

The FCF Totem

Public education was not common until the twentieth century. Therefore, many children of the eighteenth and nineteenth centuries did not have the advantage that so many children have today: a proper and balanced education. Survival in the wilderness was taught through example and word of mouth, but rarely through the written page.

Thus, many of the men who traveled the West as mountain men had little or no formal education. (It is noteworthy, however, that some mountain men were highly educated.) Many mountain men designed a totem (a simple line drawing) to indicate who they were. Look at the samples on this page.

The sample above belongs to Rick Dostal, "Simon Tanner." As you can see, he used only the *S* of the word *Simon*. Many famous mountain men and frontiersmen were named Simon, such as Simon Kenton. The rest of the totem looks like a hide being tanned, thus, "Simon Tanner."

The sample to the left belongs to Dave Erie, "Thunderhawk." If you look at the totem sideways, it contains the initials from his first and last name. When the totem is viewed as it is above, it stands for the Native American term *Thunderhawk*.

Chapter 8
Rifles and Shooting

here were two types of muzzle-loading rifles used by frontiersmen: the flintlock and the percussion rifle. The flintlock rifle used the flint and frizzen to ignite the powder in the pan, which in turn ignited the powder in the barrel. The percussion rifle used a percussion cap on a percussion nipple to ignite the powder in the barrel.

There were two general styles of rifles used by frontiersmen: the long rifle and the Hawkins rifle. The Kentucky or Pennsylvania long rifle (which was more often made in Pennsylvania) was most commonly used east of the Mississippi. However, as the frontiersmen moved westward, they needed a shorter gun to carry in the saddle. They also encountered larger game, such as the grizzly bear and the buffalo, which required a

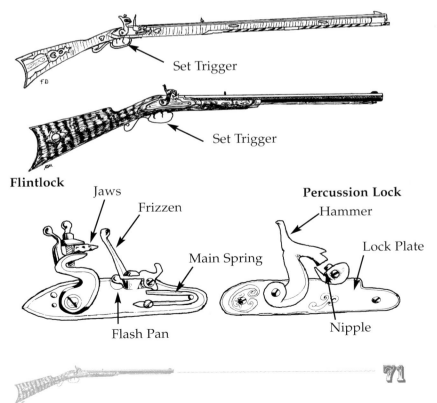

Set Trigger

Set Trigger

Flintlock

Jaws

Frizzen

Percussion Lock

Hammer

Lock Plate

Main Spring

Flash Pan

Nipple

larger caliber rifle. So in the early 1800s, a man named Jacob Hawkins developed a shorter .54-caliber rifle that became very popular with mountain men. All rifles of this style were soon called "Hawkins" rifles.

Many reproductions of these different types and styles of rifles may be purchased today. However, caution must be exercised when buying a rifle to make sure it is a good, reliable firearm. Inferior reproductions can be dangerous.

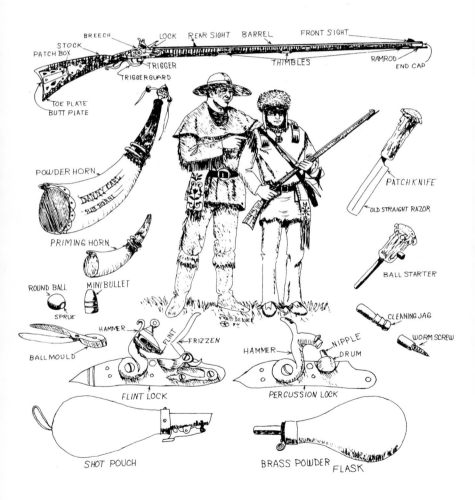

The frontiersmen who explored and fought their way across the face of our young country had to be highly skilled in all aspects of life in the wilderness. It would be difficult to say which skill was most important, but you can be assured the frontiersmen who ate well and "kept their hair" were experts in everything associated with their rifles. They knew how to shoot well, load fast, make balls, and clean and maintain their rifles. They knew how to safely handle black powder muzzle-loaders.

The purpose of this chapter is to give the basics in muzzle-loading safety and skills. The very first thing to know about muzzle-loading in FCF is that no one shoots before he has successfully completed a muzzle-loading shooters course.* This course will teach, in detail, all you need to know to correctly and properly handle a muzzle-loader. Upon successful completion of the basic muzzle-loading course, you are issued a course completion card. Show this card to your designated chapter officer, and he will issue you an official FCF shooter's card.

---

*Any NRA, NMLRA, or state-approved muzzle-loading shooter's course will qualify for the current FCF shooters card. Additional information may be obtained from the National Rifle Association of America (NRA), or the National Muzzle-Loading Rifle Association (NMLRA). The NMLRA also has advanced training courses, including a range officer school.

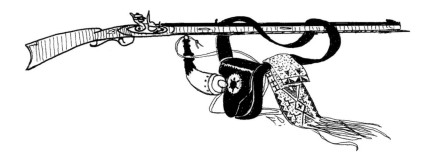

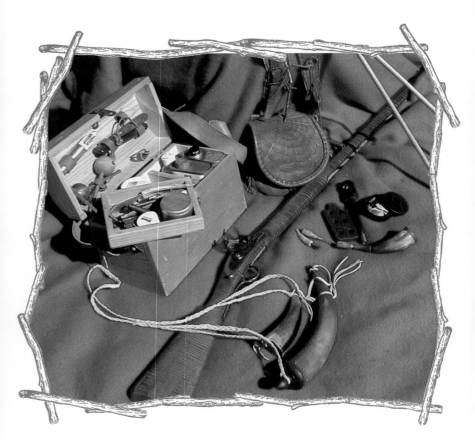

Shooting Range Rules and Commands

Royal Rangers shoot under controlled and supervised conditions on a range that has been laid out well. The various shooting events held on the range are in relays of a predetermined length of time, usually thirty minutes. These events will involve various types of targets, a certain number of rounds fired, specific types of rifles, different age groups, and anything else that can be done safely to make shooting both interesting and challenging.

Since the procedures on an official shooting range can be confusing or intimidating to new shooters, the following section will acquaint the FCF member with procedures. A well-run range is the key to having a safe and successful shoot. Please do not hesitate to ask your range officer any questions about range procedures.

1. The master range officer is in complete charge of all ranges. You must promptly comply with his or his assistants' instructions.

2. Safety is the responsibility of all shooters on the range. Careful handling of firearms and caution when moving on the range are required of all shooters.

3. While on the range, limit your conversation to official business. Loud or harassing language is not permitted.

4. It is the duty of all competitors to police the firing points and loading benches after each match. All cleaning patches, empty cap boxes, etc., must be picked up and properly discarded.

5. The command "cease firing" means to stop firing immediately. No firearm shall be discharged without permission of the range officer. Violation of this command can result in suspension of range privileges. The command may be signaled verbally or by a sharp blast of a whistle.

6. If you are not ready to load and fire, hold up your hand while calling out, "Not ready."

7. "All ready on the firing line" announces that all firing points are ready and the relay is about to begin.

8. "Commence loading—you may fire when ready" is the command that allows the shooter to load his firearm. The time of the relay starts with this command.

9. "As you were" means to disregard the command just given.

10. The question will be asked by the range officer, "Are there any hot ones?" This is to determine if any firearms are still loaded when time has expired for shooting during the relay period. If you have a loaded firearm (or a "hot one"), hold up your hand while calling out "hot one." The raised hand helps the range officer identify who has the hot one. Then the range officer will give specific instructions for discharging the load. Note also that shots for score may not be fired after the relay has ended.

11. "Make your rifle safe and bench it" means to put the hammer on the half-cock position and to uncap the nipple on percussion rifles. For flintlock rifles, open the flintlock frizzen and

place the hammer (cock) down. After the firearm has been made safe, place it in the notch of the loading bench with the muzzle pointed up.

12. When you finish shooting, make your firearm safe, bench it, and stand quietly behind the loading bench.

Loading the Muzzle-Loader

Here is a brief description of the procedure to be used when loading your muzzle-loader. This description is intended only to give a general overview.

1. Load your firearm at the loading bench only. The loading bench should be well behind the firing line.

2. To start the loading procedure for a percussion rifle, set the percussion hammer on half cock with the nipple uncapped. For a flintlock rifle, open the flintlock frizzen and place the hammer down.

3. Make sure the muzzle-loader is unloaded. Place the ramrod inside the barrel, mark the ramrod, then lay it along the outside of the barrel. For the flintlock rifle, the length between the muzzle and the touchhole should equal the length within the barrel. For the percussion rifle, the length between the muzzle and the drum should equal the length within the barrel. A patent, or hook, breech will require a small diameter rod attached to the end of the ramrod in order to reach the end of the breech.

4. Wipe the bore with a cleaning patch to remove any oil. Wipe the frizzen and flint of the flintlock. Clear the touchhole with the vent pick. Inspect the percussion nipple for obstructions, then point toward a blade of grass and snap three caps. Movement of the grass blade indicates the nipple and flash channel are clear.

5. Put the hammer of the percussion lock at half cock. On flintlocks, open the frizzen and put the hammer down.

6. Follow the manufacturer's recommendations for powder loads. If the manufacturer's instructions are not available, you can develop a rifle load. Rifles .45 caliber and larger generally use 2-Fg powder. Rifles smaller than .45 caliber use 3-Fg powder. Start with one grain of powder per caliber; e.g., .50 caliber equals fifty grains. The maximum load is one and a half times your caliber. For example, the maximum load for .50 caliber is seventy-five grains. Handguns use one-half grain of powder per caliber. For example, .45 caliber equals twenty-two and a half grains.

1. *Measure the charge of black powder*

2. *Pour powder into the clean barrel.*

3. *Press the bullet and patch into the muzzle.*

4. Trim excess patch with a sharp knife.

Use only black powder or a synthetic black powder, such as "pyrodex." Modern smokeless powder is indeed black, but it is not acceptable for use in a muzzle-loader because muzzle-loaders are not designed to take the higher pressures that develop as the modern smokeless powder burns.

7. Place the butt of the rifle on the ground between your feet. Lean the barrel in the V-notch of the loading bench or hold it between your knees with the muzzle pointing up and away from your face. Pour the powder charge into a measure from a horn or flask (see the illustration on page 78), then cap or plug your horn or flask. Pour the measured powder down the barrel. The powder is never poured directly into the barrel from the horn or flask! Tap the side of the barrel with your hand to settle the powder.

8. Place a moist or lubricated cotton or linen patch over the muzzle. Center the ball on the patch with its sprue—a small spur that remains after the lead ball has been cast—pointed up.

9. Use the short starter of the ball starter to start the ball into the muzzle. If necessary, trim the patch material with a patch knife (cutting away from your body).

10. Push the ball deeper into the barrel with the longer shaft, long starter, of your ball starter. Use a firm, continuous push.

11. Keeping the muzzle pointed up and away from your face, grip the ramrod six to eight inches from the muzzle. Push the ball down the bore with a series of short even strokes, seating the ball firmly on the powder charge but without crushing the powder or misshaping the ball. Grabbing the ramrod near its outer end or loading the ball with one stroke could snap the ramrod and cause bodily injury. If a patched ball hangs up in the barrel before seating it against the powder, pour a couple of tablespoons of water down the barrel and let it stand for twenty to thirty seconds. In this time the water will soak into the patch and loosen the fouling that caused the ball to hang. Tip the muzzle toward the ground to pour out the water.

12. With the muzzle pointed up and well above everyone's head, move to the firing line to make ready to fire the shot. When you are sure of the target—and what is behind and beyond the target—cap the percussion nipple on a percussion rifle. Prime a flintlock rifle by wetting your thumb and wiping the pan, then lightly sprinkling it with 4-Fg powder. Once the frizzen is closed, remove any visible powder. Make sure the touchhole is open. Place your feet in the shooting stance. Keeping your finger off the trigger, bring the hammer to a full cock, then shoulder the rifle. Then, as you achieve breath and sight control, slowly squeeze the trigger. Be sure to follow through (by remaining in the firing position for a few seconds

5. Push the bullet down the barrel with the starter.

6. Seat the ball on the powder with the ramrod.

7. Place the percussion cap on the nipple.

after the shot is fired). Following through is very critical when shooting a muzzle-loader because of the longer ignition time.

13. After each shot, run a moist patch, followed by a dry patch, down the barrel before reloading. A lingering spark in the barrel could ignite the next charge. Do not blow in the barrel!

Failure to Fire

A "hang fire" is a time delay in the ignition. If your rifle fails to fire, keep its muzzle pointed in a safe direction until the load has been cleared. Then, to clear the barrel, prime or cap again and fire. If this is unsuccessful, remove the priming powder or cap, clean the touchhole or nipple channel with the vent pick, prime or cap, and try again to fire. If the rifle is loaded without powder, remove the nipple from the drum with a nipple wrench. Tilt the firearm so the flash channel or touchhole is facing upward and the muzzle is pointed down. With the vent pick, work 4-Fg powder into the area behind the ball and tap the barrel lightly. Replace the nipple, reseat the ball, and prime. Shoot down range at the ground about twenty feet from the muzzle in order to see if the projectile clears the barrel.

The safest, cleanest, and quickest way to remove a load from a muzzle-loading rifle is the CO_2 ball discharger. This is the only method allowed on the NMLRA ranges. To deactivate a powder charge, remove the barrel from the stock and place the barrel breech down in at least six inches of water so it is above the touchhole or nipple. Leave the barrel in the water for half an hour or more before attempting to pull the projectile out.

Cleaning the Muzzle-Loader

A muzzle-loader can give years of enjoyable service if it is properly maintained. The single most important aspect of this maintenance is cleaning the firearm. Black powder fouling in or on a gun will cause rust to form and cause the firearm to be unusable. Therefore, it is necessary to thoroughly clean black powder firearms as soon after use as possible. Fortunately, black powder fouling is soluble in water and other cleaning agents, such as mild detergents or special solvents.

The cleaning procedure is to saturate the fouling with the cleaning agent and then wipe away the fouling a bit at a time. Solvent-wetted patches are pushed down and pulled out of the barrel until the patches come out clean. This is done by using a ramrod with a cleaning jag attached that grips the patch. This process will require the use of several patches.

The nipple or touchhole will need to be cleaned using nipple picks and pipe cleaners. The lock should be removed and thoroughly cleaned. All cleaned metal parts should be dried and oiled. The wooden stock should be protected by cleaning and applying a protective coat of wax or other suitable products. The shooter's course will cover this in more detail, but keep this in mind: There are no shortcuts that will yield satisfactory results.

Safety Reminders

1. Muzzle-loading firearms are not playthings. Treat them with the respect due any firearm.

2. Always point your rifle in a safe direction, either in the direction of the target or in the air, until fired.

3. Always wear eye and ear protection.

4. A safety shield must be placed between flintlock shooters. This will prevent injury during the firing of each weapon.

5. Make sure the downrange impact area is safe before shooting. Even though most muzzle-loaders may only be accurate to about seventy-five to one hundred yards, the ball will

travel farther downrange. You must therefore consider safety beyond the target.

6. All powder horns must be capped or closed before firing your rifle.

7. Keep your powder container closed while firing a shot, and keep it away from sparks and flames, including camp and ceremonial fires.

8. Remember, half cock on a muzzle-loader does not serve as a safety like that of a standard rifle. Even so, your muzzle-loader at half cock should not fire when the trigger is pulled. If it does, take it to a competent muzzle-loading gunsmith.

9. Use 4-Fg only as a priming powder in a flintlock, not as a loading charge.

10. Protect your muzzle-loader's ignition system during dry firing (shooting practice without actually loading). On a percussion rifle, place a faucet washer over the nipple to prevent the hammer from striking it; on a flintlock, close the frizzen. Then set the trigger and practice away.

11. Never keep a loaded firearm in camp.

12. Never use live ammunition when using your rifle in a skit.

Shooting a muzzle-loader is a truly exciting experience, one that presents a tremendous challenge. Knowledge and experience are the keys to an enjoyable shoot.

PRIME'N THE PIECE

85

Chapter 9

Powder Horns, Salt Horns, Drinking Cups

Many frontiersmen made their own powder horns, salt horns, and drinking cups out of cow or buffalo horns. They carried little food with them and used salt to season the fresh game they killed. To carry the salt, they resorted to a small cow horn, much as they had for their fine black powder if they carried a flintlock.

Many frontiersmen used a tin cup as a drinking cup. However, in many cases they made their own cups from a cow or buffalo horn; from hollow, dry gourds; or from tree burl. These carved wooden cups were called "noggins."

Powder Horn

If a frontiersman had a flintlock, he needed two horns: a small horn containing 4-Fg powder for the pan, and a larger horn with 2-Fg or 3-Fg powder for the rifle barrel. If he used a percussion rifle, he needed only one powder horn.

Commercially made powder horns may be purchased from many gun shops today. Of course, this piece of equipment will be much more special to a Frontiersmen Camping Fellowship member if he makes it himself. If he carves and engraves his horn, it will be even more valuable to him.

Making a Powder Horn

Making your own powder horn is not only enjoyable, but the results will provide a great deal of satisfaction. When beginning the project of making a horn, a couple of points need to be kept in mind. First, it's important to select a good basic horn. If you plan to engrave the horn, it should be light or white in the areas you plan to engrave. A horn with a black tip and a white body makes an excellent powder horn.

Also, if the horn is raw, you will need to boil it and clean out the membranes from inside the horn. Its exterior will need to be filed or sanded to a smooth finish. Sometimes you can buy horns that have already been cleaned and semipolished from black powder gun shops.

When you're ready to begin making the horn, here are the steps to follow:

1. Saw off the open end until you have smooth, even edges.

2. Cut off the tip of the horn and bore a small hole into the center cavity. It should be just large enough for the powder to flow freely from the horn—about the size of a matchstick (see illustration A, page 88).

3. Cut and carve a wooden plug for the large end of the horn. The plug should be about the size of the opening with a slight taper on the end. Be careful not to make it too small. The plug should have a ridge or overhang slightly larger than the opening.

4. Boil the horn until it is soft and pliable.

5. Drive the wooden plug into the end of the horn while it is still soft. When the horn cools and hardens, it will conform and seal around the plug. Grind or sand the plug to the desired shape. Secure the plug in the horn near the top edge with nails or small pegs after the horn is boiled. (See illustration B.)

6. Using hardwood or the horn tip, carve out a small plug, or stopper, for the small end of the horn. Make the small end long enough to fit well in the horn. For variety and uniqueness, carve the stopper into a shape, such as an acorn, an animal's head, or a bird's head. (See illustration C.)

HOW TO MAKE A POWDER HORN

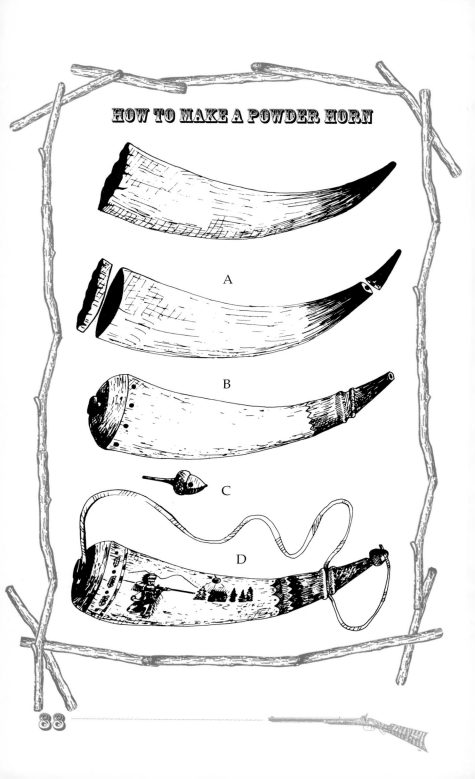

A

B

C

D

7. Sand the horn or scrape it with the edge of a piece of glass for a semifinish without polishing. You may wish to scrape down the horn so it is thin enough to see how much powder you have when you hold it up to a light.

8. Grind a groove near the small end of the horn for a leather carrying strap. (See illustration C.) If desired, carve or grind other grooves, ridges, or shapes into the horn.

9. If you wish to engrave your horn, use the following steps (referred to as the "scrimshaw" procedure):

   a. Draw the design on your horn with a felt-tipped pen. Frontiersmen drew such things as animals, birds, Native American designs, ships, and hunting scenes. (See illustration D.)

   b. Spray the design with hair spray or another fixative to keep it from smearing.

   c. With the point of a knife or other sharp instrument, etch the design into the horn.

   d. Cover the design with black ink or thin paint.

   e. Before the ink or paint has a chance to dry, wipe off the surplus, leaving only the residue in the scratch marks. This will bring out your design in bold, dark lines.

   f. You may seal the design further with a coat of wax, then polish the horn to the desired finish.

Chapter 10
Tomahawks and Knives

Tomahawks

A good tomahawk (called a "hawk" by frontiersmen) was highly prized by the frontiersman. He wore it on the back of his belt as a backup weapon (the first being his rifle). The frontiersman and the Native American alike learned to wield the hawk with deadly accuracy.

Because a tomahawk is usually affordable to every Frontiersmen Camping Fellowship member, "hawk throwing" has become one of the major events at Rendezvous and other FCF functions.

Tomahawk Throwing

It should be the goal of every FCF member to learn to throw a tomahawk with accuracy. Before attempting to learn this skill, secure a reliable tomahawk with a stout handle. Be sure the hawk head is secure on the handle before throwing it. The secret to successful hawk throwing is distance and form. A hawk must turn one complete revolution in the air before it will stick in the target. For the average-size person with an average-size hawk, seven paces is about the right distance for one revolution.

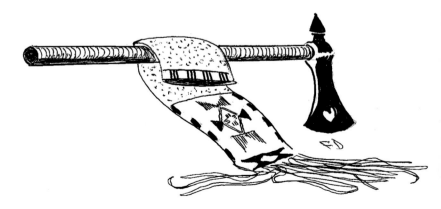

After stepping off your paces, grip the hawk firmly by the end of the handle, with the hawk blade parallel to the target. Take one step forward as you throw the hawk in an overhead swing, much as you would throw a rock or baseball. Keep your swing smooth and your wrist straight. If the hawk does not hit on the blade, adjust your pace until you find the right distance. You may also need to adjust your swing so you throw neither too hard nor too soft. Always observe basic safety rules when throwing the hawk. With practice, you can become proficient and accurate with the tomahawk.

Knives

The frontiersman used the knife as a backup weapon when the one shot in his rifle was spent. The knife came in a variety of styles, but usually was a standard skinning knife. The knife sheath was usually made from leather or rawhide and sometimes decorated with fringe, beadwork, or brass tacks. Today, some FCF members make their own knives and sheaths.

Knife Throwing

Another interesting activity that requires a lot of skill is knife throwing. It is best to use a knife that is designed for throwing. The blade of an ordinary thin-bladed knife is easily broken when thrown.

As in hawk throwing, distance and form are the keys to success in throwing a knife. However, it is much more difficult to get the right pace and form for knife throwing than it is for tomahawk throwing. In FCF, the knife is thrown by the handle only. It is thrown using an overhead swing, much as you would throw a rock.

Each individual must determine the proper distance for his knife to complete one revolution in the air before hitting the target. This varies with the length of the person's arm and the size of the knife. The individual must also use exactly the same form each time. Since the knife must hit on a small point, it takes a great deal of precision to be accurate. This skill, therefore, will require much practice.

Always remember that knife throwing can be dangerous, so be sure to follow basic safety rules at all times when throwing a knife.

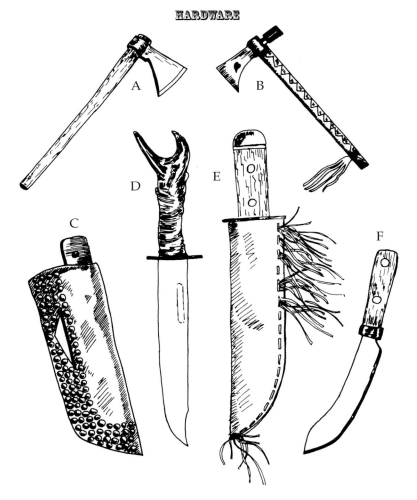

A. Throwing Tomahawk
B. Indian Trading Hawk
C. Green River Skinning Knife With Studded Sheath
D. Handmade Bone Handle Knife
E. Sheath Knife With Fringe Sheath
F. Skinning Knife

Chapter 11
Fire Starting

The early frontiersman needed the essential tools to start a fire wherever he was. He used a tinderbox, which was a small, waterproof container that carried flint, steel, and charred cloth to build a fire. Every FCF member should secure a flint-and-steel set and learn the art of starting a fire—just like our forefathers did. The secret to mastering this skill is good charred cloth, tinder, and practice, practice, practice.

Starting a Fire

Materials Needed for Starting a Fire

○ Flint or quartz

○ Steel

○ Charred cloth to catch the spark (See the instructions on charring cloth.)

○ Tinder shaped into round wads

○ Good tinder may be made from the following items:
> Inside of old bird nests
> Shredded bark of a cedar tree
> Inner bark of a dead cottonwood or basswood tree
> Fine wood scrapings
> Very dry, dead weeds or grass

Steps for Starting a Fire

To start a fire, do the following:

1. Place the tinder on the ground or a solid surface.

2. Place the charred cloth on top of the tinder. (Some prefer to place the charred cloth on the flint.)

3. Hold the flint and steel firmly with your fingers.
4. Strike glancing blows vertically against the edge of the steel, showering sparks into the charred cloth. (Some prefer to strike with the steel, others prefer the flint.)

5. When a spark is caught in the charred cloth and begins to glow, place it in the tinder.

6. Blow briskly on the charred cloth until the flame starts.

Making Charred Cloth

Materials Needed for Charred Cloth

- ○ Cotton cloth
- ○ Old cookie tin or metal can
- ○ Old shoe-polish can
- ○ Scissors
- ○ Hot plate or open fire
- ○ Eightpenny nail

Steps for Charring Cloth

1. Cut the cotton cloth into disks the same size as the shoe-polish can.

2. Place ten or twelve cloth disks in the cookie tin. Place the (metal) lid on the tin and pierce the top of the lid with a hole roughly the size of an eightpenny nail. Place the tin on a hot plate. (An open fire may be used.)

3. Allow the cloth to char until it is black. A noticeable flame will be coming from the hole in the top of the tin. The flame will disappear and some smoke will then become noticeable. Allow the tin to sit in the fire for another minute or so, then remove the tin from the heat source. (Be sure to do this outside; there will be smoke.)

4. Place the charred disks in the shoe-polish can for future use. (The can keeps the disks dry.)

Chapter 12
Shelter Building

If a frontiersman was in one place for a long period of time, he would no doubt build a log cabin. However, he usually used the same type of portable shelter as the Native Americans, such as the tepee and the lodge, when he was on the move. Primitive lean-to shelters and whitewall tents were also used by the frontiersman.

Some historians believe the tepee of the Plains Indians was one of the most ideal shelters in existence because it was lightweight and could be easily and quickly erected. By raising the side flaps, it stayed cool in summer. With a fire in the center, it stayed warm in the winter. By placing a bullboat (a shallow draft-skin boat shaped like a tub) over the top of the smoke hole, it stayed dry during a rainstorm.

We encourage Frontiersmen Camping Fellowship members to use tepees, if possible, for shelter during FCF activities. However, it does have one disadvantage; it cannot be made bug-proof like many modern tents.

If you're fortunate enough to have a tepee, you'll find the novelty of sleeping and living in this shelter takes you back in spirit to the days of the frontiersman.

Erecting a Tepee

See the illustrations below as you follow these instructions.

1. Tie three poles together to form a tripod.

2. Place ten to twelve poles evenly around the tripod, leaving space for one last pole. This will be the setting, or lifting, pole. The setting pole will be used to lift the tepee cover into place.

3. Tie the tepee to the lifting pole and lift the pole until it is standing upright.

4. Arrange the tepee over the poles, and lace it together in the front.

5. Cross two poles in the back and attach the smoke flap to them.

6. Stake the tepee down.

Chapter 13

Jerky and Pemmican

When the early frontiersman went trapping or hunting, he traveled as lightly as possible, carrying only jerky, parched corn, or pemmican for food and foraging for natural food as he went.

The first lightweight camping or trail food was jerky; then came the Native American pemmican. Both are just as nutritious and easy to make today (easier if you have a food dehydrator) as they were in the days of the frontiersman.

Making Jerky

All types of meat, including fish and fowl, can be cured, smoked, and used as traveling food by following the three-step process of soaking, smoking, and drying.

Soaking Meat in Brine

Cut off all the fat from the beef and cut it into thin slices. Soak the strips for ten to twelve hours in a saltwater solution (brine) with a ratio of one gallon of water to one pound of salt. Different flavorings can be added to taste.

Fish should be cleaned soon after they are caught. Remove the slime with a mixture of one part vinegar to four parts water. Rinse well. Cut off the heads, but leave on the tails. Try not to puncture the skin. Soak the fish overnight in brine.

Smoking the Meat

Hang the meat in the smoker for four to six hours, using only hardwood for the smoke. Remember, smoking meats only preserves and adds flavor to the meat. Meat is not cooked in a smoker. (See the illustration on page 106 for building your own smoker.)

For beef, the temperature inside the smoker should never exceed 150 degrees Fahrenheit.

For fowl, keep the smoker at 200 to 225 degrees. When the leg bone turns with ease in the socket, the bird is done.

For fish, keep the smoker above 120 degrees for two hours.

SMOKER

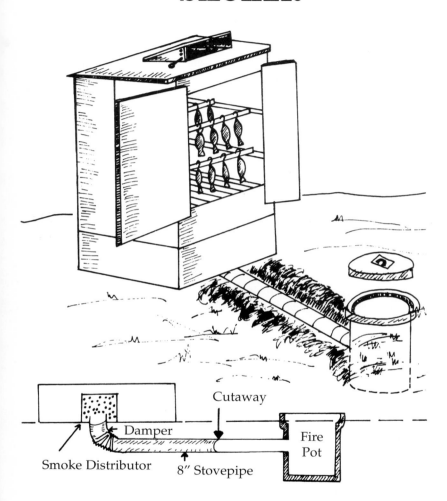

Cutaway

Damper

Smoke Distributor

8" Stovepipe

Fire Pot

Drying the Meat

Remove the meat from the smoker and place it in an oven at 200 degrees until the meat is dry—about two hours. While drying the fish, a white liquid may ooze from the surface. This is not harmful or unpleasant. It is a tasty, nutritious protein substance. Let it solidify on the surface of the fish.

Making Pemmican

Use the following recipe to make nutritious pemmican.

8 ounces Jerky (of any meat), very dry and crumbly
8 ounces Raisins
8 ounces Peanuts or pecans, unroasted
8 ounces Dried apricots, chopped (optional)
8 ounces Dried peaches, chopped (optional)
8 ounces Dried blueberries, (optional)
2 teaspoons Honey
4 tablespoons Peanut butter
3/4 teaspoon Cayenne pepper

Pound the jerky into powder or grind it using an electric blender. Add the fruit and nuts. Heat the honey and peanut butter to soften them, then blend them into the mixture. Add cayenne pepper, thoroughly working it through the mixture.

Put the pemmican in plastic tie bags. Or, if you want to go completely natural, pack it into sausage casings. Keep the pemmican in a cool, dry place. It will keep indefinitely and can't be beat as a snack or lunch on the trail!

Chapter 14

Storytelling

So here you are, an FCFer, and you want to learn about storytelling. Wah'll you done come to the right place, pilgrim, 'cause I know poor bull from fat cow. First off us profeshnulists don't call it storytellin', not allus anyways. We prefer the term spinnin' yarns.

Just about anyone can sit in front of a crowd and read a story. But it takes someone special to stand up and really tell a story. Storytelling is standing or sitting and using your voice and body language to present the story without reading from a book. A

good story has a clearly defined theme and a well-developed plot. You need to use vivid word pictures and voice variations. You must consider your audience—their ages, the types of stories they are interested in, and where the story is being told. Stories need to be brief and brought to the crowd, so get in close. Make eye contact; use gestures and facial expressions. Prepare in advance; know the theme and know your story. Learn the jargon of the era of your story. Put the emphasis on the story, not the storyteller. Dress comfortably and wear authentic outfits and costumes. Don't wear your buckskins to a pageant with Star Wars as the theme. Relax and be yourself; develop your own style.

An example is the following story written by Fred Deaver.

"A Heap o' Trouble"

A heap of trouble! Yes siree, that's what I calls 'em. Black, brown, or ol' grizzly—they be bear and that means trouble. Yep, ya can't tell stories 'bout the frontier before someone will tell 'bout how they kilt a bear or how they almost got kilt by a bear.

Now ya see, pilgrim, many years ago thar be bear everwhar ya would care to go in this great country of ours, and they was called many names. Now the Injuns sometimes called them brother, the mountain man called them grizzly, silvertip, or ol' Ephraim, and many times pioneer and Injun alike called them names we just won't mention here.

One thing fer sure, the good Lord made quite a critter when he made ol' bear. Now the bear is a large fur-bearin' animal, and he be related to the dog. When a bear walks, he steps down on the entire sole of his foot, as a man does. The bear has large, strong claws, and ol' bear can use them claws to rip a log open to git some honey, or he can use 'em to dig up ants or to catch fish. He can break a moose's back with one swat of his powerful paws.

Now ya know ol' bear's got a short tail, and also got a short temper. Ol' grizz may look clumsy or slow, but, pilgrim, bears have been known to run as fast as thirty miles an hour. I guess it be a good thing that bears hibernate; that is, they eat a lot in the summer and fall and sleep all winter.

Now most black bears usually weigh between two hundred and three hundred pounds. Although they are called black, they may be brown, light brown, or cinnamon in color.

Now, pilgrim, grizzly bears be a shade from brown to blackish

gray, and they got a big hump on their shoulders, and their hair be silvery gray. Now they may weigh as much as one thousand pounds and be ten feet tall.

But I reckon the biggest bear be the brown bear, better known as the Kodiak bear. He may weigh as much as fifteen hundred pounds and be eleven feet tall.

Well now, pilgrim, I reckon ya see now why that ol' bear can be a heap o' trouble when he wants to.

Well, sir, the Injuns and pioneers had a great respect to count "coup," that is, to touch a live bear and not kill it—or get kilt doing it. They knowed 'twere bad medicine to mess around with ol' bear. Now, pilgrim, I'll tell ya a story that goes like this.

'Bout 1828 or 1830, when they was good fur trade, and beaver skin were same as gold in yar poke, ol' Joe Meek, a mighty mountain man and free trapper, were at one of the big rendezvous—up in Yallerstone country it be. Now ol' Joe thought himself to be a mighty brave man, and were a mind to say so.

Now it seems that Joe's bravery weren't as much as another trapper thought his were. So Joe and this here other trapper got into it over which one were the bravest. It looked like thar were gonna be a shoot-out to settle the matter, when 'bout that time an ol' grizzly bear came walkin' into camp. Now, pilgrim, ol' Joe run right up to that ol' grizz, whipped out his shootin' stick, and slapped the grizz three times across his nose before he shot 'em with his big bore [Hawkins rifle]. And that ended the fussin' over who be the bravest.

Well, sir, I know you've heard 'bout ol' Dan'l Boone and Davey Crockett, and how they'd brag 'bout how they could grin a bear to death. Well now, that be truer than ya might think, pilgrim. Cause, ya see, back in them days, what with the ol' flintlock shootin' irons they had, ya had only one

HEAD'EN FER RENDEZVOUS

shot. And if'un ya just wounded or ya missed, they weren't nothin' else left to do 'cept jest stand thar and grin!

Well now, pilgrim, ya take ol' Lewis and Clark. When they went up into the Yallerstone, they told 'bout how hard 'twere to put ol' Ephraim to ground with the wepuns they carried. Seems that ol' grizz could carry more lead in his hide than a good mountain man could carry in his huntin' pouch. So it was that they stayed clear of ol' "heap o' trouble" when they could.

Well now, pilgrim, even today ol' bear is still respected—an' even feared. Many a modern-day sportsman consider the grizzly bear more dangerous than the African lion, and it might surprise ya to know that each year folks still get mauled and kilt in this country by bear.

Well now, back in the early 1800s they were a famous mountain man name of Jedidiah Smith. Ol' Jed were a leadin' some trappers up the west side o' the Black Hills when all a suddenly ol' Jed were face ta face with ol' grizz. 'Fore they could kill that bear, ol' Jed lay gashed and bleedin' with some ribs broke. Seems the bear had got ol' Jed's head in his jaws and near scalped him. With one ear tore off, ol' Jed told a feller the name of Clyman to get a needle and thread an get to sewin'. Well, sir, ol' Clyman did a right nice job stitchin'—an' a course Jed was God's mountain man—and in a little more'n two weeks Jed were up and leadin' his trappers on into Crow Injun country.

Well now, pilgrim, let me tell ya one better'n that'en 'bout Jed.

Seems they were a Major Andrew Henry leadin' some thirteen trappers fer a man name of General Ashley, head of a big fur company. I reckon it were in the spring of 1823, 'bout 150 miles out of Fort Kiowa, when a man name ol' Hugh Glass with Major Henry's party was out ahead of the rest of the trappers. When all a suddenly ol' sow grizzly with two cubs charged ol' Hugh Glass. Now ol' Glass took aim an' shot that ol' grizz sow right in the chest. But 'twern't enough to kill that ol' sow, and she caught Hugh after a short chase.

Now ol' Hugh whipped out his butcher knife and did all he could to defend hisself, but the bear near kilt ol' Hugh. It looked like Hugh were a gone goose. Everone figgered he wouldn't last that night, but come sunup ol' Hugh were still hangin' on. So Major Henry asked fer a couple of men to stay till ol' Hugh give up the ghost. Right off a young man—whose name would become famous in due time—volunteered to stay. His name were

Jim Bridger. Now another man, who were somewhat reluctant to do it, said he'd stay. His name were John Fitzgerald. Major Henry reckoned he'd pay forty each fer riskin' losin' their scalps to stay with ol' Hugh.

HEAP OF TROUBLE II

Now ol' Hugh still were hangin' on, and each day it looked like his last. Now this went on fer five days, and ol' Fitzgerald said he'd stayed as long as he were gonna. If 'un Jim wanted to keep his hair, he'd best come with him and leave Hugh. He was same as dead anyway. So it was that Jim Bridger and John Fitzgerald left Hugh Glass to die—alone. Now they took Hugh's rifle, knife, and all his fix-uns.

Well now I tell ya, pilgrim, ol' Hugh's life didn't look worth a British musket ball. But ol' Hugh didn't give up. He ate berries and drank water from a nearby spring. Now Hugh were in much pain and couldn't walk, but all Hugh could think' bout were getting even with Jim and John for leavin' him to die. Now ol' Hugh were able to kill a rattler for meat, and each day Hugh got stronger.

One day he saw some wolves that had jest kilt a buffalo calf. Now Hugh crawled up close to that kill, and fer the first time since he had been mauled by the bear, Hugh with all his strength stood on his feet and ran the wolves off with a club. Ol' Hugh survived seven weeks after the bear attack, and crawled and walked 150 miles through hostile territory back to Fort Kiowa.

Well, now, when

ol' Hugh finally found Jim, you can imagine how Jim must have felt. But ol' Hugh forgive Jim Bridger and John Fitzgerald after all, and so be it.

Well, pilgrim, ya can see why Injuns and frontiersmen wore their bear claw necklaces with pride, and a bearskin robe is mighty nice on a cold winter night. And bear meat ain't too bad if 'un that's all ya got—after all, meat's meat.

But I tell ya all, this ol' child is gonna always give old silvertip, Ephraim, and grizz the right-of-way on any trail we happen to meet! Cause ya see ol' Hawkeye aims to keep his skin in one piece, and most of all stay out of a heap o' trouble.

Advancement Sign-Off

Both Boys and Leaders

Earn the following merit awards:

	Commander's Initials	Date Completed
Rope Craft	_____	_____
Fire Craft	_____	_____
Cooking	_____	_____
Compass	_____	_____
Lashing	_____	_____
First Aid Skills	_____	_____
Camping	_____	_____
Tool Craft	_____	_____

Explain the plan of salvation to a commander.
Date Completed _____

Explain the meaning of the RR emblem.
Four Red Points   Date Completed _____
Four Gold Points   Date Completed _____
Eight Blue Points   Date Completed _____

Boys Only

Are you an Adventure Ranger?   YES
Date of your eleventh birthday   _____

Leaders Only

Ranger Basics module   Date Completed _____
Are you a RR leader in good standing with your church?   YES
Your Signature _____
Pastor's Signature _____

Both Boys and Leaders

You are now eligible for the Frontier Adventure. After successful
completion, you will receive your Frontiersmen Pin.

Both Boys and Leaders

Earn the following merit awards:

	Commander's Initials	Date Completed
Church	_____	_____
Knife and Hawk	_____	_____
Black Powder	_____	_____
Or		
Archery	_____	_____

Frontier Adventure   Date Attended   _____

FCF outfit made or purchased?	YES
FCF Pledge memorized?	YES
Meaning of the FCF Symbol explained?	YES
Vision and purpose of FCF stated?	YES
FCF identification staff made?	YES

Frontier-related craft or skill: _____

FCF name: _____

Buckskin chapter of
the FCF workbook   Date Completed _____

Active member in good standing for one year?   YES

Boys Only

Bronze Medal
Or
Expedition Ranger Medal   Date Earned_____

Leaders Only

LMA   Date Earned _____

Name of boy sponsored into FCF: _____

_____ .

Both Boys and Leaders

   Submit your application for advancement to Buckskin to the district FCF office. After successful completion of the Buckskin testing, you will be awarded your Buckskin Pin.

WILDERNESS

Both Boys and Leaders

Earn the following merit awards:

		Commander's Initials	Date Completed
	Christian Service	_____	_____
	Wilderness Survival	_____	_____
	Primitive Snares	_____	_____
	Primitive Shelters	_____	_____
	Wilderness chapter of the FCF workbook	_____	_____

Boys Only

Silver Medal
Or
Second Expedition   Date Completed _____
   Ranger Medal
Name of boy sponsored into FCF: _____
Frontier Adventures (2)   Dates Attended _____ _____
An active member in good standing for at least two years?   YES

Leaders Only

National Training Camp   Date Attended _____
Name of second boy sponsored into FCF: _____
Frontier Adventures (4)   Dates Attended _____ _____
                                                      _____ _____
An active member in good standing for at least two years?   YES

Both Boys and Leaders

   Submit your application for advancement to Wilderness to the district FCF office. Then wear the Wilderness Pouch until the Vigil is completed. After successful completion of the Wilderness Vigil, you will be awarded your Wilderness Pin.

God's Word for Our Handbook

As you read each chapter of this handbook, read the corresponding Scripture verses. These verses will help you keep in mind the spiritual significance of the Frontiersmen Camping Fellowship ministry.

"The History of FCF," page 12
   1 Corinthians 1:9
"The FCF Motto," page 13
   Luke 6:38
   John 13:16
"The FCF Symbol," page 13
   Luke 3:16
"The FCF Pledge," page 14
   Romans 12:10
"The Organization of FCF," page 25
   Proverbs 3:5,6
"Steps of Recognition in FCF," page 30
   Psalm 75:6–7
"The Trappers Brigade," page 35
   Mark 12:31
   Galatians 6:2
"The Pathfinder," page 41
   Psalm 27:11
   Mark 16:15
"The Frontiersman's Outfit," page 53
   Ephesians 6:10–18
"Leather and Beads," page 63
   2 Kings 1:8
"Identification Staffs and Totems," page 67
   Psalm 23:4
"Rifles and Shooting," page 71
   2 Corinthians 10:4
"Powder Horns, Salt Horns, Drinking Cups," page 86
   Matthew 5:13

"Tomahawks and Knives," page 91
   2 Corinthians 6:7
   Hebrews 4:12
"Fire Starting," page 97
   Luke 12:49
"Shelter Building," page 101
   Psalm 31:20
   Psalm 61:3,4
"Jerky and Pemmican," page 105
   Psalm 78:25
"Storytelling," page 109
   Matthew 28:15
Additional Scripture: God's Blessings
   Numbers 6:24–26

Glossary

Achievement: One of five important qualities to be demonstrated by FCFers. Achievement is one of the logs of the fire in the FCF emblem.

Beaver or Child: Terms used for a person, either for oneself or someone else, not a derogatory term.

Bourgeois: This is the second step in the Trappers Brigade. It is received after earning sixty points.

Buckskin: The second level of achievement in FCF. This is typically the time in which the FCF member receives his FCF name.

Buffler: Buffalo. The favorite food of the trapper and Native American.

Buffler Wood: Buffalo chips, dried buffalo dung. Used for fuel in cooking fires.

Bushway or Booshway: From the French word *bourgeois*. A company man who supervised indentured trappers who were forced to work for a fur trapping company. At the buckskinner's Rendezvous these days a booshway is the person in charge of a Rendezvous.

Chapter: The name of the FCF group within each district. For instance, the Southern Missouri District is the Daniel Boone Chapter.

Company Man: An employee of a fur trapping company, looked down upon by the free trappers.

Company Trapper: The first step earned in the Trappers Brigade. It is received after earning twenty points.

Courage: One of five important qualities to be demonstrated by FCFers. Courage is one of the logs of the fire in the FCF emblem.

Diggins: Home.

FCF: Frontiersmen Camping Fellowship.

FCF Motto: To Give and to Serve (Latin: *Ad Dare Servire*)

FCF Name: Usually during the Buckskin ceremony, the inductee is given or chooses a name that demonstrates a special skill, personal description, etc.

FCF Pledge: States the purpose and principles of FCF.

FCF Symbol: A blazing campfire fueled by five logs: friendship, leadership, woodsmanship, achievement, and courage. There are three parts of the flame: Christian love (warmth), personal witness (light), and dedicated service (usefulness).

Feedbag: Eating a meal, also the stomach or abdominal area of the body.

Feeling Right Pert: Feeling pretty good.

Flatlander: Term of contempt for someone who was "green," or new to the mountains.

Flint and Steel: Method used by the mountain men to start fires. See the chapter entitled "Fire Starting."

Flintlock: A black powder rifle that uses a flint to ignite the powder, which launches a bullet from the barrel.

Foofurah, Fo Farrah, Foo Furaw: Trinkets, trade goods, doodads, bells, and mirrors, etc. From the French word *fanfaron*. Every trapper carried a supply of these items as trade goods.

Fotch: To knock or hit another man, like in a fight.

Free Trapper: The ultimate mountain man. A trapper who was his own boss. A free man who was not indentured to or working for a fur trapping company. It is also the highest step in the Trappers Brigade and is received after earning 120 points.

Friendship: One of five important qualities to be demonstrated by FCFers. Friendship is one of the logs of the fire in the FCF emblem.

Frontiersman: The first advancement step in FCF. See the chapter entitled "Steps of Recognition in FCF" for further information.

Greenhorn: A term to describe the inexperienced newcomer to the mountains.

Green Is Weared Off: When a greenhorn becomes a mountain man.

Hawk: A tomahawk.

Hawkins: The typical black powder rifle owned by the mountain man. It had a shorter barrel and forestock than a Kentucky rifle.

Heap: Plenty of something.

Hole: A secluded mountain valley.

Kentucky Long Rifle: A black powder rifle that was widely used during the mountain man and frontiersman era. It had a long barrel and a forestock that extended to the end of the barrel.

Leadership: One of five important qualities to be demonstrated by FCFers. Leadership is one of the logs of the fire in the FCF emblem.

Lodge: Home. The title given to the primitive shelters that FCF members use for camping. These include tepees, wall tents, baker tents, pyramid tents, and many others.

Old (Ole) Hoss: A term to describe someone. ("Bill, you ole hoss, I hain't seed you since last ronnyvoo!")

Old-Timer: Refers to FCF members over the age of eighteen.

Palaver: A corruption of the Portuguese word *palavra,* meaning "to talk."

Parfleche: A rawhide for making containers, moccasin soles, shields, and a type of suitcase. It is usually decorated with painted designs.

Pathfinders: A program that provides the opportunity for FCF members to provide assistance to those who might otherwise not receive help from standard MAPS teams or missionary workers.

Paunch: The stomach or meat bag.

Pemmican: An Indian word for pounded, dried meat combined with dried berries or currants, mixed with melted fat, and stored in cakes. It could be eaten as it was or turned into a rich soup by adding water and heating it over a fire.

Percussion: A black powder rifle that uses a cap to ignite the powder within the barrel.

Pilgrim: Someone new to the mountains. Much the same as "greenhorn" or "flatlander."

Pirogue: A canoe made by hollowing out a log. A French word.

Plew: A beaver pelt, from the French word for "plus." Also, the Hudson's Bay Company used to mark each "made beaver" or pelt with a "+" in their accounting ledgers.

Possibles: A small, but highly important collection of valuable items the trapper kept with him in his shooting pouch or "possibles bag", which could mean the difference between life and death when put afoot without a rifle. (Read *The Saga of Hugh Glass: Pirate, Pawnee, and Mountain Man* by John Myers.)

Rendezvous: Historically, a meeting place of mountain men during the 1820s and 1830s. It was an annual summer get-together when the trappers came down out of the mountains to trade furs, swap gossip, and generally have a good time. This was also the time when the trappers would buy supplies for the

coming year in the mountains. Only eight rendezvous were held in the Green River setting, with a total of sixteen that occurred in the Rocky Mountain area. These were held annually from 1825 until 1840, except for 1831 when the supply wagons failed to arrive on time. Two minor rendezvous were held in the 1840s, with the last being held by Jim Bridger in 1843 near his fort. Today, Rendezvous refers to an event held every four years at the national level and every two years in the territories.

Ronnyvoo or Rondyvoo: Rendezvous.

Scout: This position is held by a Young Buck for two years. He is selected by FCF members during chapter traces or Rendezvous.

Shoot Center or Plum Center: A trustworthy rifle or a bull's-eye.

Sign: Anything that tells the trapper something about the country he's in.

Sky Pilot: A preacher.

Slik as Shootin: Something done very well by trapper standards.

Sours My Milk: Upsets me.

Take a Horn: Take a drink.

Territory: The name given to each region. For instance, the North Central Region is called the Explorers.

Totem: A graphic depiction of the FCF name of an FCF member. Many mountain men were illiterate, so they often resorted to drawing pictures to indicate who they were.

Trace: A special yearly event that encourages Old-Timers and Young Bucks to develop more skills and to experience God's creation in a rugged, outdoor environment.

Trappers Brigade: An advancement system developed to promote Christian service among the FCF members.

Trek: A challenging hike/trip taken to demonstrate the abilities of each FCF member in the most primitive of settings and with the least amount of conveniences.

Voyageur: French for "traveler." A French-Canadian canoe handler. They were thought of as cowards and held in contempt by the free trappers.

Waah! Waugh! Wagh!: An exclamation of surprise or admiration that sounds like a grunt. A common sound of the grizzly bear.

Wilderness: The highest achievement in FCF. The requirements can be found in the chapter titled "Steps of Recognition in FCF."

Woodsmanship: One of five important qualities to be demonstrated by FCFers. Woodsmanship is one of the logs of the fire in the FCF emblem.

Young Buck: Refers to FCF members between the ages of eleven and seventeen.